A STOLEN LIFE

SEARCHING FOR RICHARD PIERPOINT

A STOLEN LIFE

PETER MEYLER   DAVID MEYLER

NATURAL HERITAGE BOOKS
TORONTO

Published by Natural Heritage/Natural History Inc.
P.O. Box 95, Station O, Toronto, Ontario M4A 2M8

Cover photo by Peter Meyler
Design by Blanche Hamill, Norton Hamill Design
Edited by Jane Gibson
Printed and bound in Canada by Hignell Printing Limited

Canadian Cataloguing in Publication Data

Meyler, Peter
    A stolen life : searching for Richard Pierpoint

Includes bibliographical references and index.
ISBN 1-896219-55-1

1. Pierpoint, Richard, 1744?-1837.   2. Canada—History—1763-1791.
3. Canada—History—1791-1841.   4. Africans—Ontario—Biography.
5. Blacks—Ontario—Biography.   6. Black Canadians—Biography.*
I. Meyler, David.   II. Title.

FC3100.B6M49 1999   971.3'00496'0092   C99-931719-9
F1059.7.N3M49 1999

THE CANADA COUNCIL | LE CONSEIL DES ARTS
FOR THE ARTS | DU CANADA
SINCE 1957 | DEPUIS 1957

Natural Heritage/Natural History Inc. acknowledges the support received for its
publishing program from the Canada Council Block Grant Program. We also
acknowledge with gratitude the assistance of the Association for the Export of
Canadian Books, Ottawa.

Dedicated to John Meyler and Anna Meyler-Visser who taught us that the world belongs to everyone.

Acknowledgments

We would like to thank John and Anna Meyler, Pat Mestern, Ted Weber, the Ontario Heritage Foundation and all those who made donations for their help with the commemoration plaque project which was the impetus for this work. We would also like to thank the staff of the Orangeville Public Library for their help in retrieving a number of resource materials. We would like to acknowledge the Archives of Ontario, the Robarts Library at the University of Toronto, the Toronto Reference Library, the Wellington County Museum and Archives, the Dufferin County Museum and Archives, the Northumberland County Historical Society, the St. Catharines Museum and the Norval Johnson Heritage Library in Niagara Falls for their excellent resource materials. Thanks to Alston Fraser for his help with the cover photo, to Jon K. Juppien of St. Catherines and to all of the many individuals who provided information and guidance during this long project.

While we have made every effort to ensure the accuracy of the information in this book, we would gratefully receive any corrections or suggestions which will be incorporated in future editions.

Contents

Introduction

Merchant houses sit peacefully on the northeast side of Gorée Island, belying the tragedies that they have seen. Gorée was the main slave trading centre for the French off of the coast of Senegal. Holding quarters for African captives who were to be shipped to the main fortress across the harbour, are found on the lower level of these houses. At the back of the houses are small doorways along the water's edge which were used to receive small craft which ferried cargo to and from the mainland. The people of Senegal call them "the doors of no return."[1] In 1983 we learned of a man from Senegal who had been one of those who never returned.

We grew up just outside of a small "Scottish" town in southwestern Ontario. The local history told of lowland Scots being the first settlers in 1833, the year the town of Fergus was founded. We had never heard of any African settlers during our school years. In 1983, however, a two volume local history was published to commemorate the town's sesquicentennial. It contained a section on the "Pierpoint Settlement," a settlement of Africans that was here before the Scots had arrived. It came as quite a surprise to learn that there had been black pioneers living along the Grand River where we had spent much of our childhood playing. Their story had been left out of the history either through ignorance or prejudice. The mythology that has evolved depicts Canadian history stemming from two founding races, the French and the British; and this is what was taught in our schools. Other European nationalities who were here were barely mentioned in the textbooks, let alone African pioneers and settlers.

In 1994 we undertook a project to erect an historical marker for Pierpoint in front of John Black Public School, the school we had attended from grades 1 to 8. The school which is in the Glen Lamond area of West Garafraxa Township sits in the middle of what was Pierpoint's property. When we started the project, we assumed that the information on Pierpoint would be fairly complete. However, when we looked at the available research and the writings, we found many inconsistencies and assumptions. These included the existence of the Pierpoint settlement itself and the burial place of the old African. The portrayal of Pierpoint was also inconsistent. The Canadian Biography listing paints Pierpoint as a downtrodden figure, while the oral history in the black community indicates that he had a leadership role in the province.

After the plaque had been erected, we decided to continue our research. Here was a story that deserved to be known, after all Pierpoint was personally involved in the African slave trade, the Seven Years War, the American War for Independence and the War of 1812. His role, like other Africans in the northern British colonies, is not fully understood by most people. The role of Africans who chose to stay with the British after the American Revolution ended is even more unknown. By following Captain Dick, as Pierpoint was later known, through his long life we hope to portray the places and times that he encountered, and thereby gain a sense of the kind of man he was and of the contributions that were made by Africans in the early settlement of North America.

We have subtitled the book *Searching for Richard Pierpoint* because very little first hand information is available in the historical records. Tracing Richard Pierpoint's life has been like chasing shadows, seeing a shape or an outline, but never clearly seeing the full dimension of the figure. For this reason, much of his life can only be surmised from the stories and circumstances of other Africans in North America, and from the historical context of the times.

The truly amazing fact about Captain Dick is that we know of him at all. It is for this reason that it is important to let as many people as possible to learn about him. In this way, the shadows left by other Africans in North America may also be seen.

Where possible, excerpts from relevant documents are used to support and enhance our understanding of the context. Such material has been left in its original form, with the spelling, grammar and general sentence structure untouched.

1   The Wellspring

Turquoise waters rolling in from the Atlantic Ocean cascaded over the sand. News, by word-of-mouth, message or signal, spread quickly into the interior. Sails had been sighted on the horizon. A merchant ship was coming to port. Suddenly, the flow of goods on the hinterland trade routes accelerated.

In 1760, on the west coast of Africa, among the more valuable commodities for sale were humans. In small groups or in long coffles, a sort of living train of shackled and yoked prisoners was forced to carry other trade goods. These slaves for market were brought to the factories, the European trading ports that dotted the coast; the French were on the lower Senegal at Gorée, the British on the Gambia at Fort James and, further south, were the Dutch and Portuguese.

Slavery as a social phenomenon was not unknown to the west Africans, but the European "chattel" slavery was a new and destructive form, destructive both for individuals and whole societies. Like much of the trans-Atlantic slave trade, we have no exact number of the people involved. Estimates range up to 22 million, of which only half survived the ordeal of capture, confinement and transport to the Americas.[1]

But for the most, they are anonymous, faceless victims. We know, however, much in general: how they were captured; the conditions of the trans-Atlantic voyage; their living conditions. Only in a few cases do we have an individual biography, where the special circumstances needed came together to allow for the preservation of one person's unique story. First-hand published accounts include those of Ayuba Sulayman Diallo, a nobleman of Bundu, and Olaudah Equiano of the Ibo people in Nigeria. Alex Haley's painstaking work has revealed the story of Kunte Kinte, a Mandinke of the Gambia River. Only through these stories can we put a true human face on a tragedy that otherwise threatens to overwhelm us with its magnitude.

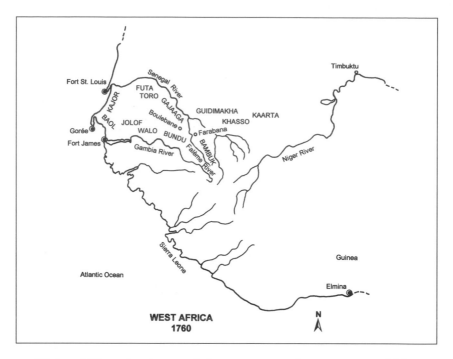

Richard Pierpoint is one of the rare cases where a personal history is recorded, but it is only through the survival of a single document, a petition from 1821, that we could begin to reconstruct his life. In the petition, Pierpoint, then more than 75 years old, gives his life story in a brief few lines: "That your excellency's petitioner is a native of Bondu in Africa; that at the age of sixteen years he was made a prisoner and sold as a slave; that he was conveyed to America about the year 1760, and sold to a British officer..."[2]

Bondu, or now more commonly given as Bundu, is a key clue, as is Pierpoint's age, so we can at least locate him with fair specificity in a particular place and time. It is especially noteworthy that Pierpoint gave Bundu, located in what is now eastern Senegal on the border of Mali, as his birthplace instead of a town or village. It is a more sophisticated concept of citizenship, in an age before modern nationalism, than would have been found in most places around the globe. In Europe at this time, most people would still be more likely to associate themselves with their home town or province rather than a national state. This is the case with Kunte Kinte, where the last element is less a surname than an indication of his home village, Kunte

from the village of Kinte. In later life, Pierpoint's contemporaries
thought Bondu in fact referred to a town.

Ayuba Sulayman Diallo (the Arabic form of Jacob (Job Ben)
Solomon) had returned to Bundu in 1734, after being freed from slavery in Maryland by British benefactors. He belonged to the generation before Pierpoint, but through Ayuba's detailed narrative we can
see the kind of society in which the young Richard spent his first 16
years.[3] The history of Bundu dates back to the fall of the Songhai
Empire in the late sixteenth century. This was the last of the great west
African empires south of the Sahara which grew rich on the cross-
desert trade routes. Songhai collapsed due to a variety of reasons,
including both a devastating invasion by Sultan Ahmad el Mansur of
Morocco in 1591 and the growing European slave raids from their
coastal enclaves.

The Moroccans, well equipped with muskets, met the Songhai
army, led by Askia Ishak, near Lake Chad in the Battle of Tondibi in
1591. The Songhai forces, based on bow and spear armed cavalry,
charged the Moroccan ranks. But their quilted coats and metal
armour covering both man and horse, while adequate for stopping
an arrow or blunting a sword cut, were no protection against the hail
of musket shot produced by the Moroccan foot soldiers. Contemporary chronicles also strongly suggest there was treachery within the
royal Songhai family.

The eclipse of the armoured horseman as the dominant force on
the battlefield, having succumbed to technology and superior tactics,
can be seen as a metaphor for the eclipse of much of traditional society in Songhai Africa. Although the Moroccans did not stay as
conquerors, heading back north across the desert with their booty, the
ruling Askia dynasty in Songhai was discredited and, already suffer-
ing from serious internal differences, was fatally weakened as a political and military force.

A collapsing Songhai proved equally incapable of stopping European incursions. Starting with the Portuguese, and followed by the
Dutch, English and French, European trading bases were established
on the coast. New east to west trade patterns, from the interior to the
coast, supplanted the traditional trans-Saharan routes. With this, the
vital commercial sinews of the empire were torn apart.

The net effect was a time of political chaos as a whole series of new,
small states arose on the broken foundations of what had been Song-

hai. The coastal regions soon came under European dominance, if not outright control. But inland from the coast, a number of permanent states developed, supplying the Europeans with the trade goods they desired from the interior: various raw materials such as gum; luxuries such as gold and ivory; and above all, slaves.

The Fulbe people, known variously as the Fulani, Pholey, Peul, Toucouleur or Fula (depending on the era and geography), were one of the most widespread of the many ethnic groups that had lived under Songhai rule. Their language is called Pulaar. The origins of the Fulbe in distant prehistory are not known, but over generations they had probably migrated from north and east of Lake Chad towards the Atlantic coast. They were traditionally a nomadic, pastoral people of the Sahel, the border region between the Sahara and the southern forests, whose wealth was measured in ownership of humpbacked, long-horned cattle. As a borderland people, their physical appearance and customs demonstrated the shared influences of the peoples both north and south of the Sahara. The Fulbe had settled in a broad cres-cent-shaped area stretching from what is now Nigeria to the Senegal River. By the time of Ayuba, many Fulbe had settled in towns and had converted to Islam. However, the majority remained as pastoralists living in small villages, and many of these retained their traditional religious practices. By the late seventeenth century, three Fulbe states had been established in the Senegambia region. To the north, on the Senegal river, was Futa Toro, while in the highlands south of the Gambia was Futa Jallon. In between was Bundu, strategically located between the lower Gambia and Senegal rivers.

Bundu had its origins in the last quarter of the seventeenth century, when a certain Malik Sy settled in the sparsely-populated southern portion of the Soninke Gajaaga state. A native of Futa Toro, Malik was a member of the Torodbe, a kind of clerical caste. While the origins of this group are unclear, the Torodbe may have been manumitted slaves and thus excluded from most of the profes-sional or tradesmen castes; they devoted themselves to religious studies and mercantile activities. Malik himself was an Islamic scholar of renown. By the time he, his extended family and assorted followers moved to Gajaaga, and joined up with a number of other unrelated Fulbe migrants, the population was large enough to form a number of villages politically dominated by an Islamic clergy. The Sy family, Sissibe in its plural form, provided the nascent state with some political permanence through the formation of a kind of theocratic dynasty. At the same time, southern Gajaaga provided the permanent territorial base.

Bundu itself is a non-Pulaar word, meaning "well."[4] In Fulbe tradition, a person who cleared some land, or dug a well (in other words made the land agriculturally productive) gained title to that land. The implication here is that the rulers of Gajaaga, for whatever reason, had neglected to ensure the productivity of this region and had, therefore, forfeited their rights to it, rights usurped by the Sissibe. How exactly Malik Sy gained title is unclear, but folklore hints of some subterfuge. Nor was the Sissibe right to rule unchallenged among the other Fulbe nobles in the community.

Regardless, the Fulbe did not come as conquerors. From the beginning, Bundu was an ethnically diverse state, based on the cooperation of the new arrivals with the original inhabitants (who probably saw the arrival of Malik Sy as an opportunity to break free from the rule of the dominant Gajaagan towns in the north). These inhabitants were largely Soninke, but there were also smaller populations of Mandinke and Wolof. However, during the early 1700s, there had been a dynastic civil war, but Bundu survived as a distinct state and, by 1730, the Sissibe family were again in power.

Malik Sy and his followers ruled as absolute priest-kings, under the title of eliman (from the Arabic al imam) but with power somewhat limited by a council of nobles. The kingship was elective through the council of nobles, although only members of the royal Sissibe line were eligible to rule. There was no rule of primogeniture, where the eldest son automatically inherited the crown, and, as the Muslim nobility tended to have more than one wife, the number of royal heirs could be substantial. This would later cause political instability, but for the time period included here, the Sissibe ruled a politically unified and stable realm. In spite of being ruled by an Islamic theocracy, the non-Muslim population, and this included most of the Soninke many of whom were just nominally Muslim, as well as a portion of the Fulbe themselves, held full rights in the state and their local customs were respected.

To the immediate north of Bundu were the Soninke states of Gajaaga, straddling the Senegal River, and Guidimakha to the east. These were of some of the oldest states in the region. Gajaaga was essentially a federation of a number of large semi-independent

The ostrich feather in his turban indicates that this Fulbe was a commanding officer. An officer was also distinguished from regular troops by his blue clothing.

commercial towns and smaller political centres. The latter were ruled by a warrior class, while the towns were dominated by wealthy merchants. There were a number of kings called tunkas, with a paramount tunka chosen from among them. The power of the tunka was limited and dynastic struggles were a constant threat to the stability of the state. Malik Sy had probably used such a period of weakness to establish his realm. In any case, Bundu would not hesitate later to interfere in Gajaagan dynastic disputes. Guidimakha, a collection of dispersed farming villages with a few trading towns, had no central government at all and it, in particular, suffered from Moorish slave raids. It thus, inadvertently, provided a shield for Bundu against all but the worst of these raids. To the west, were the largely non-Muslim Wolof states of Kajor Baol, Jolof and Walo, but Bundu apparently had little significant interaction with them.

RULERS OF BUNDU	1698-1764
MALIK SY	1698-1699
BUBU MALIK	1699-1715
INTERREGNUM	1716-1720
MAKA JIBA	1720-1764

The situation to the east was quite different. Here were the relatively powerful states of Bambuk and Khasso. Khasso, a partially Islamized state, with a mixed Mandinke-Fulbe population, occupied both sides of the upper Senegal. It was ruled by a Fulbe royal family, but dynastic disputes would weaken Khasso's power, and see much of its territory lost to the new Bambara kingdom of Kaarta, established in the early 1750s. Bambuk, a non-Muslim Mandinke state, was a mountainous wedge of land between Khasso and Bundu. The relatively small population was dispersed in numerous, independent villages. The various villages, while never able to form a permanent alliance, would cooperate in mutual defence. This support and the rugged terrain allowed Bambuk to maintain its independence against its more powerful neighbours. It was not Bambuk's relatively poor soil that attracted the attention of invaders, but the rich gold deposits at or near surface level.

Although its boundaries would vary, Bundu occupied a core territory of 33,000 sq. km., with a population of perhaps 30,000. The west of the country was comprised of the Ferlo, an arid plain of sparse grasslands, shrubs and lonely stands of trees. Towards the south, the climate is humid and hot, with rolling hills and dense vegetation. Moving north and east, the land flattens out into a more arid plain, eventually blending into the Ferlo wilderness. The most fertile region was to the east, along the valley of the Faleme River, a major tributary of the Senegal, green with trees and rich with crops. Bundu has two seasons, a dry winter and rainy summer (lasting May to November, but shorter in the north). Annual rainfall ranges from 100 cm in the south to 40 cm in the lower Senegal valley.

Bundu occupied a strategic crossroads on the trade routes from the interior to the coast. Trade was the life blood of the state. Domestically produced trade goods included: cattle, millet, rice (where the climate allowed), groundnuts and cotton (both raw and woven cloth). Whether it was Bambuk gold, Bundu cotton and captive slaves being shipped to the coast, or European firearms, Indian textiles and rum coming upstream along the Gambia or the Senegal, most goods had to come through Bundu. The rulers of Bundu also played the British and the French off against each other, as goods could either be shipped down the Senegal to the French post of Saint Louis, or down the Gambia to the British Fort James.

This brief overview shows Bundu's role in the varied and thriving life of the Senegambian basin, after the fall of Songhai and during the first phase of European settlement. The daily life of the people of Bundu, while varying in some details from one community to another, shared many general characteristics found throughout west Africa. The Fulbe, Soninke, Wolof and Mandinke were all stratified societies. There were three broad classifications: freemen, caste groups and slaves. But each of these groups was further divided into many subgroups, with the top members of the caste and slave categories having more wealth and influence than the lower levels of freemen. Included among freemen were: the nobles, farmers, herders, fishermen, along with Muslim traders and clerics. Non-Fulbe could hold noble status, but this was rare.

Caste groups were usually based on occupation: griots (a combination praise singer, historian and musician); blacksmiths; woodworkers; leatherworkers; potters and so on. Occupations and status were passed down from father to son (at least among the Fulbe who had switched from a matrilinear to patrilinear form of inheritance when they converted to Islam).

The caste groups held an ambiguous position. While not considered a part of regular society (it was not considered appropriate for freemen to marry a member of a caste), blacksmiths and griots often formed close patron-client relationships with the ruling elite and could have much influence. Woodworkers (trees were considered the resting place of spirits) and leatherworkers (who worked with dead animals) both violated strong taboos and were shunned as potential sources of evil.

Except perhaps in size, rank was seldom evident through construction of buildings. The type of clay soil in this region of west Africa does not lend itself to brick making. Walls are usually built of mud reinforced with wooden poles. Even royal palaces and mosques used this traditional and distinctive building method. Houses in towns were usually square and flat roofed. Rural villages would have round mud-walled

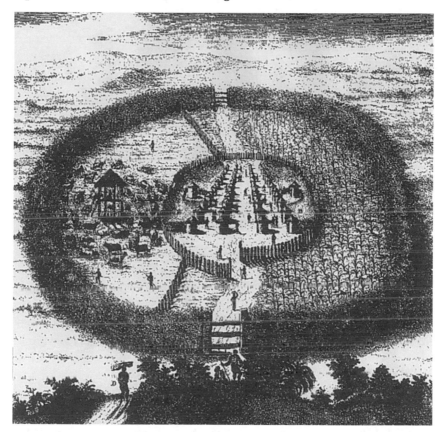

Some of the typical agricultural activities were carried on in this Fulbe village. Corn, cotton and cattle were raised inside the village enclave. Groundnuts were another major agricultural crop for Bundu and is still a major export commodity for Senegal today.

houses with a conical pole roof covered in thatch, or alternatively, the entire structure would be made of vertical wood poles, but with a similar conical thatched roof. Contemporary illustrations from the time of Ayuba Sulayman show a typical village with its circular dwellings laid out in an orderly street pattern. The village is surrounded by a circular stockade of poles, with one open gate. Outside the stockade are millet fields and an enclosed pen for cattle. The whole is enclosed again by a thick hedge, with two closed gates.[5] Pierpoint would see a somewhat similar form of town planning in North America among the traditional palisaded villages of the Six Nations.

The most common type of clothing was made of the white cotton woven by the Fulbe themselves. But the Wolof were the acknowledged masters of cloth weaving, famous for their bright blue and yellow dyes. Aside from a flowing kaftan or tunic, a traditional form of clothing for both men and women was made out of two lengths of cloth. One would be used as a wraparound skirt like a sarong or kilt, while the other length would be draped around the shoulders like a kind of toga. Turbans were the common headgear for men. Women often wore their hair in intricate braids.

The slave or servile class shared some similarities with the serfdom of feudal Europe, and mirrored some aspects of slavery in classical Rome. (It should be noted that some west African states had no slavery.) Most slaves were captured in battle, although debt could also force a freeman to become a slave. Domestic slaves were rarely beaten. In rural areas slaves would farm their own small plots, giving up a share of the produce to their master. Kinship systems were paramount in Bundu as elsewhere in west Africa and, without the protection of a clan, slaves were most vulnerable in the immediate period after their capture. Once integrated into a village or clan, however, the prospects of ill-treatment or being resold declined sharply. As European demands for slaves increased, Bundu was one of the number of states, probably facing a threat of depopulation, that forbade the sale of their own citizens as slaves.[6]

While all young men were liable for military service, many ruling dynasties in west Africa also relied on a small corps of servile warriors, acting as both a standing army and a royal guard. As slaves, they owed allegiance only to the ruling family, and had none of the clan affiliations that made other armed troops politically unreliable. Similarly, most royal servants were also slaves and, as in ancient Rome, these

royal slaves could hold immense wealth and influence as trusted coun-
cillors. Even family members, with their own dynastic claims, were
not as trustworthy as a politically neutral slave.

Islam tended to provide a unifying element that cut across clan affiliation, ethnic origin or language. Schools were maintained by Muslim
clerics and all boys, whether or not they were Muslim, attended them,
from around seven years of age to adulthood (up to 15 years of age).[7]
Here they would learn some basics of reading and writing in Arabic,
numeracy and Islamic custom. Schooling for girls was less formal,
with the focus on household and farming chores. All in all, education
was on par or superior to that found in most of the world at the time.
Age-grades also cut across clan affiliation. All children entered adulthood at the same time, usually between the ages of 12 and 16 (often
there were stages of initiation). All boys of the same age would be liable
for military service. Pierpoint's age of capture, 16 years, may be significant and the age-grade system is likely the reason why he knew his
age. Perhaps, while on a raid outside Bundu or defending against
attack, Pierpoint, a young and possibly inexperienced warrior in his
first combat, fell victim to capture.

As much of Pierpoint's life would revolve around military
service, it is relevant to take a closer look at the army of Bundu.
The Sissibe dynasty provided the means, both in terms of resources
and long-term interest, for a standing army. The expansionary drive
of early Bundu provided the need. The core of the army was a
permanent force of slaves, that numbered from 400 to 1000 depending on time and circumstance. For times of emergency, civilians
were liable for military duty, with each free family required to
provide one fully equipped soldier (sometimes more). Conscripts
had four days to report. Villages which failed to provide their quota
were liable to be pillaged by the eliman's slaves. The call for duty
was done in one or more of three ways: Sissibe nobles themselves
would travel from village to village to personally appeal for aid;
royal slaves would cross the country bearing the message; or drums
would be used to beat out the signal for a call to arms. While the
primary duty of the standing army was to guard trade routes, the
garrisons were kept at the main towns of Boulebane and Koussan.
The army was also used to patrol restive borders and to garrison a
chain of permanent forts (called a tata), kept along the southern and
eastern frontiers.

Omaribn Sayid was a native of Bundu's neighbouring state of Futa Toro. This image of Omaribn was taken in 1828 when he was a slave in North Carolina and a practising Muslim.

The most important force was the mounted arm. The eliman was responsible for providing horses for his personal entourage and his body-guard of courtiers, relatives and slaves. The permanent garrisons, at least, were trained in battlefield manoeuvres. The army was subdivided into smaller tactical units, commanded by the sons and brothers of the eliman, and all of whom were expected to lead from the front. The officers wore blue as a distinguishing feature and, as a further mark of rank, wore an ostrich feather in their turban. The commanding general wore three such plumes. Firearms were the most important weapon, but conscripts were often equipped with just a spear and bow. We can only speculate as to what social class and ethnic group Pierpoint belonged. The majority of the population were Fulbe farmers and herders, and it was this class that provided the bulk of the conscripts for the army.

Capture in battle and kidnapping by slave raiders were the two most common ways an individual could end up enslaved. Kidnapping appeared to be relatively rare inside Bundu, as its centralized government and fortified garrisons provided a high degree of security. Mandinke villages along the Gambia were more vulnerable. Alex Haley's subject, Kunte Kinte, went into the woods to collect wood and was never seen again, kidnapped by slavers. His family never knew his fate. But leaving Bundu could be hazardous. Ayuba Sulayman, travelling along the Gambia with a herd of cattle to sell, ventured too far into unfamiliar Mandinke territory. He not only lost his cattle to a band of Mandinke slavers, but also his own freedom. If a family was wealthy enough, knew what had happened and acted promptly, a captive relative could be redeemed. Once sold to a European trader, however, there was little chance of getting back home. Ayuba's father was almost in time to save his son from the trans-Atlantic journey, but Ayuba was one of the fortunate few slaves to return to his homeland after being shipped across the ocean.[8]

In a present-day Fulbe village, such as this one, a griot may be telling the story of the disappearance of the 16-year-old we know as Richard Pierpoint. A griot can recount a family's history for hundreds of years.

Pierpoint lived during the long reign of the eliman Maka Jiba, who ruled from approximately 1720 to 1764. Maka Jiba restored the Sissibe family to power after the dynastic civil war in the second decade of the 18th century. By the time Pierpoint was born, around 1744, the domestic situation in Bundu was stable. The main foreign threats came from the Moors, Futa Toro, Gajaaga and the Bambuk town of Farabana. The Moors, represented by the Ormankobe slave raiders, were a serious plague for much of Maka Jiba's reign, even if Bundu was not usually a primary target. However, the Ormankobe were only interested in capturing slaves for their own army, not for resale. As well, the worst of the raids had ended by 1750, although sporadic attacks continued until 1764. But, had Pierpoint been captured by the Ormankobe, he would have disappeared north into the desert. It is more likely that he was captured by one of the other enemies of Bundu.

Between 1747-51, Futu Toro, which looked upon Bundu as a vassal state, undertook a major campaign against it. Initially successful, the Futu Toro army would suffer heavy losses in a second battle and eventually retreated. This war, however, was over almost a decade before Pierpoint said he was captured, around 1760. Sometime after the war with Futu Toro, a prolonged struggle began with Gajaaga. Bundu was allied with Khasso, while the Gajaagans used Bambara mercenaries from the newly formed state of Kaarta. Overall, this conflict was fought at a low level of intensity. Stimulated in part by the prospects of increased trade with the British, and in part by a desire to have a more secure hold over the gold supply and the slave caravan routes, Maka Jiba began a long-term war of expansion against Farabana. Farabana was one of the main Bambuk towns in the Falème valley and, by controlling a number of neighbouring satellite villages, it formed a small city state. The fighting was prolonged, indecisive and would outlast Maka Jiba himself who died in 1764.

While not directly affecting Bundu, a civil war in the Wolof state of Kajor Baol could have had some spill over effects. In 1757, Dyolof Birayanb took over the kingship of Kajor driving out his rival, Maysa. Kajor usually traded with the French, but Biryanb refused to deal in slaves. Between 1758-63, Maysa made a successful comeback and killed Biryanb at the battle of Mbal. From that time onwards, 250 slaves a year were delivered to market.[9]

One other major event affecting Pierpoint's life was the Seven Years War of 1756-63, one of the first modern world wars with fighting in

North America, India and Africa. Between May and December of 1758, the British took the French bases of Fort St. Louis and Gorée, effectively shutting the French out of the west African slave trade. The French bases would not be returned to them until 1783. Before 1758, if Pierpoint had been a victim of a Gajaaga-Bambara raid, he would have been sold along the Senegal River, and thus end up in the French slaving network. Capture by Farabana would probably have seen him sold down the Gambia to the British. In 1760, however, he ended up as a captive, there was only one end destination: a British slave port on the Atlantic coast.

2   The Time of Terror

Terror on the face of Richard Pierpoint and the other newer arrivals to the slave caravan was understandable. Being captured as a slave was tragedy enough, but while there might be many different languages spoken among the captives, one horrific rumour in particular was prevalent, that the Europeans were taking Africans to eat them. What else could be the reason for such a great demand for human flesh? The Europeans, aside from a small number kept around the trading bases, did not use the captives as soldiers, for farming or for labour, all the things an African slave might expect. Thousands disappeared each year on the great ships and none ever returned. Some even said that the Europeans, with no land of their own, were permanently adrift on their huge vessels and survived through cannibalism. There is a sad irony here. Stories of cannibalism among the "savages" of the African interior became the stock and trade of the accounts of European travellers, although these spurious tales ring particularly hollow when one thinks of the level of sophistication among the states of Senegambia.[1]

If the slaves did not have to face cannibalism, what they did have to endure was little better. Long marches to the European trading posts were followed by incarceration in holding pens or dungeons. On the Gambia, the main British base was Fort James, situated on a river island, but smaller, semi-permanent satellite posts, called factories, dotted the river as far upstream as navigable traffic allowed.[2] Along the Senegal River, slave trading occurred mainly between July and November when the rains raised the river level enough to allow river-boats passage to Gajaaga, one of the slave trading areas. The whole process from capture to sale on the slave market could take months.

If there were a large number of slaves to be moved, they were formed into a coffle or slave caravan. Already they may have spent months or even years in captivity. Strings of 30 or 40 people were tied together by leather thongs around their necks or by wooden yokes and shackles. The captives carried a load of grain, ivory or other trade goods, as well as water and food for their own provisions. If there were no goods to transport, at times captives were made to carry rocks, their resulting exhaustion likely to lessen the risk of escape. Coffles heading for the coast were particularly prone to escape attempts and, those caught, were forced to wear a heavy wooden shackle about a metre in length. Some slaves would attempt suicide as their only viable escape. Whippings were a common occurrence to keep the caravans moving at a good pace. Sick or injured slaves, if there was a chance of recovery, would be carried along rather than abandoned and thus becoming a loss of a profitable piece of merchandise.

Some captives attempted to keep up their spirits through singing, a practice encouraged by the slave drivers, but most were described as dejected, sullen and apathetic. Disease, injuries, maltreatment, all these would have already taken their toll by the time the caravans reached the river trading posts. If there were no buyers immediately available, or if a price could not be agreed upon, the slaves would remain at the post, bound in heavy chains or used for labour there. Slaves acquired on behalf of the Royal African Company and its successor, "the Company of Merchants Trading to Africa," would be shipped down and held at Fort James until a full shipload had been gathered. An independent merchant would have to keep his slaves aboard ship, sailing along the coast until a sufficient number had been bought. With sanitary conditions in both the fort and the slave ships rudimentary, and the whole process taking months, infectious diseases were prevalent. Ghost ships were not unknown where the entire cargo of slaves and crew had been killed off by an outbreak of some malady, yellow fever being one of the most dangerous.[3]

It was still in the best interests of the joncoes, the slave brokers, to keep their captives in as good as health as possible to obtain the maximum price. A captive's hair would be closely shaved to hide any grey that might indicate old age, and his or her skin would be glossed with palm oil, while a calculated dose of rum or other spirits would help soften a sullen or depressed attitude. But it took a clever broker to fool an experienced slave merchant at the auctions, especially if he was aided by a surgeon. Slaves would be made to perform various types of exercises to show their level of agility and

Captured men were shackled together in irons to prevent resistance while travelling to the slave ship. Many were kept in shackles for the ocean voyage and when brought on deck for the forced daily dance could only jump up and down as their chains rattled.

stamina. Breathing would be noted and teeth, which could show the victim's true age and state of health, were checked for wear. The slaves were stripped naked and carefully inspected for any signs of infectious disease, one more humiliation, and one especially distressing for Muslim women.[4]

As a boy of 16, Pierpoint was typical of most slaves captured, since young males were preferred. The average age of slaves taken from Africa was 14 years. Younger slaves were, of course, easier to manage than adults, and still had most of their prime working years ahead of them. Thus, it would not be inaccurate to call the trans-Atlantic slave trade an industry based on the exploitation and sale of children.

Even if a healthy and full cargo of slaves was secured, the merchantman was not safe. Shipboard slave revolts were not common but did happen should the crew be unwary. A more common danger was the many raids by coastal Africans. These could either be by kinsmen attempting to rescue their family or by pirates, the latter being more common. If a merchant vessel was successfully stormed and taken, the hapless captives would simply be resold again, or kept as slaves by their

Ayuba Sulayman Diallo (Jacob Ben Soloman) survived
the trek from Bundu and the Atlantic crossing in 1731.
The son of a cleric, Ayuba wrote a letter in Arabic that
eventually went from his plantation in Maryland to
England for translation. As a result of the letter he was
able to gain his freedom and return home.

new captors. Once a ship cleared the coast, and the Africans only view
was of the relentless ocean and endless sky, such dangers diminished.

In 1750, the British parliament had enacted legislation reforming
the Royal Africa Company, ending its monopoly and providing
freedom of trade for all "His Majesty's subjects" along the coast
from Morocco to the Cape of Good Hope. The newly-created
"Company of Merchants Trading to Africa" was incorporated as a
regulated company, with shares open to purchase from any interested trader. The Company acquired all the forts, settlements and
territories held by the now-dissolved Royal Africa Company.[5] The
most important difference between the new and the old company
was that agents responsible for administering the forts and posts

were prohibited from trading on their own behalf. Otherwise, there was fear the Company employees would have an unfair advantage over the other merchants.

However, this proved a contentious issue almost as soon as the bill was passed. By 1760, private trade by the agents of the Company was not only tolerated, but even encouraged. It was found that slave traders who arrived at a post and found no immediate buyer would frequently move on to a French, Dutch or Portuguese post. This private trade, as it was termed, was thus designed to keep the slave trade in the British system if no other merchants were on hand. Abuses did occur, where Company agents illegally sold slaves to foreign merchants, these same French, Portuguese or Dutch.[6]

In the legal trade, most slaves bought by Company merchants were shipped to the Caribbean, even if they were destined for the American colonies. Here, the slaves would be "seasoned" on the sugar plantations in Barbados and Jamaica. This was a process that could last several years while captured Africans would be acclimatized to their new surroundings and duties. It also allowed the slaves to become healthier and learn some rudimentary English before they were sold. Africans who were not sold in the Caribbean would be shipped north to the main American slave markets in Charleston, New York or Boston, while newly arrived captives took their places. Conditions in the Caribbean were so brutal that, for slaves in the American colonies, shipment to the sugar plantations was often used as the ultimate form of punishment for repeated escape attempts or other serious forms of insubordination.

In Britain, the slave trade was controlled by the merchants of London, Liverpool and Bristol. But the ports of the American colonies supported their own small slave trading enterprises, and most of the captives shipped directly to the colonies were carried by these independents. The following is the text of letter written by one such merchant, Timothy Fitch, to an employee, Captain Peter Quinn, dated January 12, 1760, in Boston, Massachusetts:

"Sir you having the command of my schooner Phillis your orders are to imbrace the first favorable opertunity of wind & weather & proceed directly for the coast of Affrica, touching first at Sinagall if you fall in with it on your arrival then cum to anchor with your vessel & go up to the Facktory in your boat & see if you can part with any of your cargo to advantage . . . if you could sell the whole of your cargo there to a good proffett & take slaves & cash viz. cum directly home . . . You must spend as little time as possible at Sinigal & then proceed down the coast to Sere Leon & then make the best trade you can from place to place till you have disposed of all of your cargo & purchase your compleat cargo of young slaves which I suppose will be about 70 or eighty more or less I would recommend to you gowing to the Isle of Delos if you cant finish at Sereleon . . . be sure to bring as few women & girls as possibl . . . hope you wont be detained upon the coast longer than ye 1st of May by any means, the consequence you know e have experienced to be bad, You & your people & slaves will get sick which will ruin the voyage. Whatever you have left upon hand after April, sell it altogeather for what you can get even at the first cost rather than tary any longer . . . be constantly upon your gard night & day & keep good watch that you may not be cutt of by your own slaves tho neavour so fiew on board that you are not taken by sirprise by boats from the shore which has often ben the case Let your slaves be well lookd after properly & carefully tended Kept in action by playing upon deck . . . if sick well tended in ye half deck & by all means keep up thare spirretts & when you cum off the coast bring off a full allowance of rice & water for a ten week pasage Upon this your voyage depends in agrate measure . . . by all means I reacommend industry, frugality & dispatch which will reacommend you to further bussiness. Your wages is three pounds ten sterling per month three slaves, priviledge & three % but of the cargo of slaves delivered at Boston, This is all you are to have . . ."[7]

The routine of life was the same on most slave ships, a result of trial and error to achieve the maximum profit with the minimum effort. The slaves were fed twice a day, brought up on deck in groups of ten around the mid morning and the late afternoon. Larger groups could prove dangerous to manage. Adult men were brought to the main deck where they were closely watched by armed crewmen. Women ate on the quarterdeck with the crew, while children were taken to the poop or stern deck. Slave food consisted of a gruel made from rice, maize or "horse beans." These latter beans were shipped specially from England and were considered a good cure against diarrhoea, no small concern considering the poor diet. Water, a pint each, was the main drink. When within sight of the coast, escape attempts became possible, so slaves were only allowed up to use the lavatories. These were simple planks with holes, about 12 in row, fitted to over-hang the deck of a ship.

Once well out to sea, slaves could be allowed more freedom of move-ment if weather allowed, but misdemeanours were dealt with harshly, from floggings to mutilation and even execution for those who were unredeemably insubordinate. Weather in the middle Atlantic was the main risk a slaver faced. Storms could sink a vessel outright, of course, but any significant delay in arriving in port could have just as fatal results. The image of the slaves packed like sardines in a can is well known and, even if not all slave ships were packed so tightly, it was still the aim of the slave traders to load as many people as possible on board. A 100-ton merchant vessel would usually carry a maximum of 200 to 300 slaves, but the ratio could be as high as one captive for every one-fifth ton of displacement or more, depending on the greed of the trader. Even so, conditions below decks in the holds were abysmal at the best of times, with small port holes providing minimal ventilation. In times of bad weather, when all ports had to be shut and the slaves could not be brought above deck for any reason, sanitation would deteriorate to health-threatening levels. The stench was said to be indescribable. Slave ships could often be smelled before they were seen.[8]

A British inquiry into the slave trade by the Committee of the Privy Council in 1789 reported that the mortality rate in slave ships had dropped, from almost 25 percent around 1700 to ten percent by 1734. But these are averages. Some slaves ships made the crossing with few losses, while others could be lost at sea with all on board. But, by 1760, when Richard Pierpoint made his crossing, slavers had established a routine that ensured the bulk of their cargoes could be brought to market with an acceptable loss of life, acceptable compared to the worst slave voyages of the preceding two or three generations.[9]

The site of the American coast on the horizon signalled the end of the terrifying journey across the Atlantic. But a new terror gripped the Africans trapped on the stench-filled ship. The time to find out if the story that these strange white people ate their captives was true was approaching; this supposition created a great deal of terror among these Africans. To allay this fear and help reduce the incidence of riots and rebellions, slave traders brought older, experienced African slaves on board. They would explain to the captives, in their native languages, that they were to be sold as slaves and would only be put

Yarrow Mamout, a resident of Washington, D.C., lived to be over 100 years old. A practising Muslim, he probably came from the Senegambia area of Africa.

to work in this new country. Olaudah Equiano, one of the Africans to write an autobiography, described his experience this way: "we were to be carried to this white people's country to work for them. I was then a little relieved, and thought if it were no worse than working, my situation was not so desperate."[10]

As the port of destination was approached, the slaves were prepared for market. Disease, either contracted before or during the voyage, had to be hidden from the prospective buyers. Rubbing down the skin with bizarre mixtures of oil, lime juice and gun powder, sometimes mixed with iron rust, was said to be effective in hiding the telltale signs of the yaws, a very common and contagious skin disease. For each trick the slaver came up with, however, the equally clever slave buyer would come up with a counter. Nevertheless, it was estimated that a

third of the slaves from any particular shipment would be dead within
three years from the yaws, or its often equally destructive treatments.
Smallpox was another major killer of slaves, weakened from the cross-
Atlantic passage.

Around 1760, the 16-year-old African who would become Richard
Pierpoint, would have been learning of his fate as his ship docked at
an American port. He had seen his share of horror on the ocean
voyage, but obviously he was one of the survivors. What innate skills
or characteristics could he draw upon to adapt and survive in his new
circumstances, now impossibly far from family and home? Here, Pierpoint's ethnic origin may provide some clues. To date, there has been
little study in the ethnic origins of slaves, but we do know that Fulbe
slaves were uncommon in the British colonies. The British took most
of their slaves from Ghana and Nigeria, farther south from the Senegal and Gambia rivers. Even in the Senegambia region, the Mandinke
were the most frequent victims. In part this was due to the fact that
the French, before 1759 and after 1783, controlled most of the slave
trade along the Senegal River, thus, most Fulbe captives would have
ended up in the French trading network. The British victory in the
Seven Years War, then, created one of the few periods when a significant supply of Fulbe captives would have been available.

There are other clues. European commentators said Fulbe considered themselves superior to non-Fulbe. In Bundu society, the Fulbe
nobility, in particular, and Fulbe freemen, in general, held a superior
position to non-Fulbe.[11] This was more by custom than by law, and
Bundu had one of the most pluralistic communities of the region. In
his later life, Pierpoint, or "Captain Dick" as he was called by his
contemporaries (and this showed he was considered to have some
kind of assumed authority over his fellow Africans, though he never
held any official military rank above private soldier), would take on
leadership roles. In the 1790s he sought to form an all-African community and, later, did form an all-African military unit in 1812. Did a
Fulbe heritage give Pierpoint the pride and confidence to take on such
pretensions? It is possible.

Pierpoint now had to make a new life for himself. If military misad-
venture had led to his capture, it was the military again that would
help define his new identity as Richard Pierpoint.

3   A Piece of Property

Pierpoint could have been sold in any of the slave markets in the northern British colonies. He indicated in his 1821 petition that he was bought by a British officer. It was common practice for officers to "commandeer" their required servants from the rank and file, but it was also common practice for the gentleman officer to buy a slave for his personal servant. In fact, by 1781, during the American Revolution, the critical shortage of recruits in the British army made taking men out of the line a serious drain on trained soldiers, and a law was enacted to require officers to use only slaves as their personal servants. Even earlier, this particular officer would have needed a personal servant to help in his activities during the war, known as the French-Indian War, that had been going on between the British colonies and the French from Canada. A teenager of 16 or 17 years would be a preferred age for this for this type of buyer, the slave was mature enough to be responsible but young enough to be trained effectively.

We do not know for certain if Pierpoint was Fulbe, but a significant clue is his purchase by the British officer. The Seven Years War was still in full swing in 1760, and no officer, whether serving in the regular or colonial forces, would be without a personal servant. The appearance of a personal slave served as a status symbol for the owner. A good-looking, smartly dressed servant was as much part of an officer's suite as his scarlet uniform, bedecked with gold braid and lace trim.

There were several factors contributing to the preference for Fulbe. Fulbe tended to be tall and, to European eyes, were more attractive, possessing more refined features and fairer skin, than their Mandinke and Soninke neighbours. Dr. Collins, in a guide for slaveowners, wrote that natives of Senegal could be distinguished from other nationalities by their features which resembled "the whites" and "their tall and well limbed bodies."[1] His guide also included this advice: "They are excellent for the care of cattle and horses, and for domestic service though little qualified for the ruder labours of the field, to which they never ought to be applied."[2]

After docking, slaves were sold privately or at public auction. Stark black and white notices would be posted and advertisements placed, extolling the benefits of a particular lot of human cargo. The July 29, 1761, Boston papers advertised such a shipment of Africans. The ad offered for sale: "A parcel of likely Negroes from Africa, cheap for cash or short credit; Enquire John Avery , at his House, next Door to the White-House, or at a Store adjoining to said Avery's Distill-House, at the South End, near South Market; Also, if any Persons have any Negro Men, strong and hearty, tho' not of the best moral character, which are proper Subjects for Transportation, may have an Exchange for small Negroes."[3]

Naked, tired, scared and confused, the human property would be displayed to their prospective purchasers. They would be poked and prodded, have their teeth checked, and be inspected for any physical

Slave auctions were a regular part of life in port cities throughout the Americas. Families were often separated since buyers might need only one slave or be looking for a servant with particular skills or attributes. In 1761, seven year old Phillis Wheatley was sold in Boston after arriving from Senegal on the slave ship *Phillis*.

defects. They would be made to jump, twist, bend and dance to show that they were in good shape and that their joints worked properly. Haggling would carry on until a suitable price was established. Some clothes would be provided to the newly bought slave and then, shackled or tied, they would be led away to their life of servitude.

Connecticut may have been where Pierpoint first arrived in the northern colonies. In 1774 there were over 16,000 blacks in this colony. Slaves quite often took or were given the last name of an owner; one of the prominent families in Connecticut was the Pierpont family.

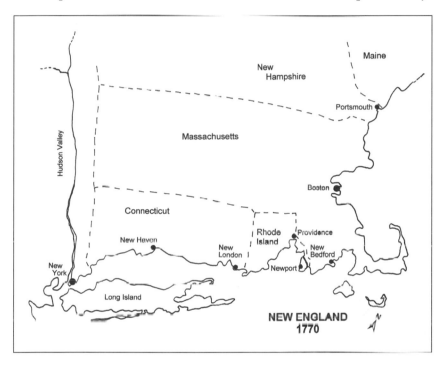

While the original spelling of the name in England was Pierrepont, in New England the name had been shortened to Pierpont although variations of spelling did occur, including Pierpoint.

The first Pierpont arrived in the 1600s and lived in Roxbury, Connecticut. By 1760, the family had members in various locations in Connecticut as well as in other colonies. There were no Pierponts listed on the regular army lists of this period, however, a number of members of the Pierpont family of New England did serve in the colonial militia. They would have been embroiled in the French-Indian

War between France and England along with their Native allies. Jacob
Pierpoint was such a soldier, having fought with the 2nd Regiment,
6th Company from March 29, 1760 to November 20, 1760. He later
joined the winter company of Captain Fitch and died on April 1, 1762.
During the American Revolution, many of the colonists had switched
loyalties and became Patriots. Included in these was Captain John
Pierpont whose ship was captured during the revolutionary war, and
Robert Pierpont who was a member of the Boston Committee of
Correspondence in 1774. Any one of these could have been young
Richard's buyer As for the first name, Richard or Dick was a usual
enough slave name.

No matter who his purchaser was, the teenaged Pierpoint was
enmeshed in an amazing state of change in his life. Not only was he
separated from his family, but he was in the midst of a completely
foreign culture, with strange foods, customs and language. His new
surroundings also were astoundingly different, the forests of the
Atlantic seacoast and the harsh winters created a stark contrast to the
sunbaked soil of his homeland.

The Joshua Hempstead House is situated in the centre of New London, Connecticut. A minor slave port during John Butler's boyhood in the city, it had a large
African population at the time. The area around Hempstead House was home
to many of these colonial African Americans.

Many newly-arrived Africans experienced depression during their enslavement. This was most evident when they first arrived. Olaudah Equiano described his feelings after his arrival in Virginia: "All my companions were distributed different ways and only myself was left. I was now exceedingly miserable and thought myself worse off than any of the rest ...for they could talk to each other, but I had no person to speak to that I could understand."[4]

Chloe Spear recalled that she wished she were dead when she arrived in Boston in 1762. Suicide was a frequent occurrence during the middle passage or after arrival in America. For many, death meant a return to their homeland. In her memoirs, Chloe Spear compared this belief with the arrival of the new moon after the demise of the old moon. She wrote, "...the first child born into a family after the decease of a member be the same individual come back again."[5] If, however, Pierpoint was a Muslim, the idea of suicide would be contrary to his religious beliefs and his faith would have had to sustain him.

Around 1760, the young Pierpoint was entering this world of despair and confusion. Most African slaves in New England and New York lived in close proximity with their masters, quite often in the same house. Pierpoint's first communication with his master would have been with gestures and signals. Some simple English would have begun to be taught and, if he was lucky, there may have been other Africans in the family who would help with this process. His new duties would have been taught by example, a time consuming task for both the teenaged African and his master since communication was so difficult. Much of the training must have involved military procedures and care of the military materials used by the British officer to fulfil his duties. Pierpoint's training would have required a sense of duty and discipline since an officer's servant would go into battle with his master. These qualities were not always valuable characteristics in slaves; such traits might lead slaves to throw off the sense of inferiority that was necessary for maintaining their state of slavery.

Pierpoint's background might have already included military service in Bundu, equipping him with experience in the art of warfare. Many natives of Bundu were excellent horsemen, and modern weapons had been traded by the Europeans for African goods since trading began between the two continents.

After the fall of the city of Quebec in 1759, the British prepared their final assaults on the remaining French strongholds. Four thousand British regulars arrived at Montreal on September 5, 1760. A second army assembled at Crown Point on Lake Champlain and sailed against the French at Ile aux Noix. Ten thousand more left Oswego and sailed down the St. Lawrence to eliminate French resistance between Lake Ontario and Montreal. Among the British troops were a large number of militia from New England and New York. On September 8, the French governor general of Canada, the Marquis de Vaudreuil, surrendered Montreal and the remainder of New France to the British.

Richard Pierpoint might not have been involved in any actual combat during the French-Indian War. However, after the major hostilities ended, troops were needed to maintain the peace that finally came to the northern colonies, duties that were mainly handled by colonial militia. Most of the British regular troops were sent to other areas of conflict with the French, for the Seven Year's War, of which the French-Indian War was a part, continued around the world until 1763.

The withdrawal of these British regulars led to an economic depression in the colonies, especially affecting the coastal areas. No longer were British soldiers and sailors around to spend their pay on local goods and services. The British government no longer needed the housing, food and equipment that had supplied their forces. Everyone, from farmers in the back country to ship builders in the port cities, was adversely affected. Pierpoint's master would have been hurt economically by the loss of this military commerce as well. With this loss and no longer a need for a personal servant for military duty, it may have been shortly after the end of the war that Richard was sold again. Where he lived at this time is unknown, but it would have been in the northern colonies.

Even though there were only a few slaves in most homes, they managed to keep some of their African customs and beliefs, a practice that would have given some relief to Pierpoint's culture shock. At the time most Africans in the north were concentrated in certain centres. By 1776, New York City's population was over twenty percent African. In 1774, almost half of Connecticut's blacks lived in the commercial centres of New London and Fairfield, while in Massachusetts half of the colony's Africans lived in the Boston area. At the time of Pierpoint's arrival about half of the black residents were born in the Americas while the rest were natives of Africa.[6] These people continued to hold African beliefs and practised their customs, even if such were hidden under a European guise. Pierpoint would become an integral part of this growing African-American culture in the northern British colonies.

The most important beliefs held by slaves were those related to religion. In New England there was no great zeal for converting slaves to Christianity since there were spiritual conflicts involved with the concept of a Christian being a slave. Reverend John Sharpe, a military chaplain in New York described the prevailing white attitude in a 1713 publication:

> "...the Negroes were much discouraged from embracing the Christian religion upon account of the very little regard showed them in any religious respect. Their marriages were performed by mutual consent only, without the blessing of the Church; they were buried by those of their own country or complexion in the common field, without any Christian office...No notice was given of their being sick that they might be visited; on the contrary, frequent discourse were made in conversations that they had no souls and perished as beasts."[7]

At the time of the American Revolution only three percent of Africans in Newport, Rhode Island were Christians in good standing, while another twenty-five percent may have attended church at one time or another.[8] Africans did not readily try to adopt Christianity. The version practised in the northern colonies was very staid and book-oriented, while Africans were much more attuned to experiential religious practices. When slaveowners did teach any Christianity to their slaves, they generally used Bible passages that confirmed the validity of slavery. A native of Africa was unlikely to embrace a religion that approved of a position that, to the slave, was fundamentally unjust. It is unlikely that Pierpoint became a Christian during his time of slavery.

Two basic religions were brought to America from Africa, the traditional beliefs and Islam. While the majority of Africans would have followed the old spirit-based practices, a smaller group would have followed Islam. In this group there would have been both strict practitioners of the religion and those that followed the basic tenets, but did not follow all of the Islamic laws.

A folk religion, blending various facets of different beliefs, developed since there was a mixture of various African nationalities in the northern colonies. Aspects of European beliefs, such as witchcraft, charms, evil spirits and ghosts which were familiar to Africans, were added to the blend. The addition of these convictions added validity, from the white colonists' perspective, to the religious practices of Africans and would help to nullify any criticism or harassment. A slave master in Barbados wrote that the slaves were: "...very tenaciously addicted to the rites, ceremonies, and superstitions of their own countries, particularly in their plays, dances, music, marriages and burials."[9]

It was the general practice not to teach slaves to read or write. Slaves were much easier to control when as many ways of communicating as possible were eliminated. This was especially true for communications that could used over long distances and for those that could not be understood by Europeans. For this reason, African drumming was not allowed in many areas. Slaves also were not allowed to speak their own languages. Equally, writing was discouraged, often with punishments for those who learned without the approval of the master. Such punishments could include the sale of the slave or the cutting off of fingers.

People of the same ethnic group would be separated to prevent any "secret" talk, but it is likely that newly-arrived Africans would seek out and make contact with fellow countrymen. A favourite meeting place was at the Sabbath day markets. At a central location, the women would continue their traditional marketing practices and bring goods and produce such as corn and apples to trade and sell. In addition to the economic benefits, the other important function of these markets was the chance to socialize. For the men it was also an opportunity to share a drink with friends and to play games. Paw paw, gambling with cowrie shells, was a favourite pastime. It eventually passed into European society in the north and became one of the most popular games in New England.[10]

Another feature of African gatherings was music. Many men were trained musicians, even though their white masters thought that they had acquired the talent to play instruments *naturally*. Favourite instruments were violins and flutes. Sometimes, drums could be incorporated into the music, but only if they were presented as toy drums. Often black fiddlers were used at white dances because of their skill and energetic style of playing. The combination of African rhythms mixed with those of Europe created the new sounds of the colonies.

Africans did not take their captivity for granted. Some managed to buy their freedom by earning money through selling products or being hired out. Others, escaping into the hinterland, were taken in by the

Natives. Runaway slaves were not always destitute. In fact, those with resources may have been more likely to try an escape. An advertisement for the recapture of Charles Roberts, also known as German, included this description of the young man:

> "He has a variety of Clothes, some of them very good, affects to dress very neat and genteel, and generally wears a Wig. He took with him two or three Coats or Suits, viz. A dark brown or chocolate colored Cloth, of fine Frize, but little worn; a dun or Dove colored Cloth, of fine Frize, pretty much worn; and a Summer Coat, of Grogham, Camblet, or some such Stuff; a Straw coloured Waistcoat, edged with a Silver Cord, almost new; and several other waistcoats, Breeches, and Pairs of Stockings; a Blue Great Coat, and a Fiddle. His behavior is excessively complisant, obsequious and insinuating; he speaks good English, smoothly and plausibly, and generally with a Cringe and a Smile; he is extremely artful, and ready at inventing specious Pretences to conceal villainous Actions or Designs. He plays on the Fiddle, can read and write tolerably well, and understands a little Arithmetick and Accounts."[11]

The position held by German was probably similar to Pierpoint's original position of service to the British officer. Pierpoint also may have dressed in the style of this description.

Revolts by groups of Africans in the northern colonies, often with Natives as allies, were not uncommon. These acts led to new laws that tried to further control African freedom. Connecticut had a law, even though it seems to have been rarely enforced, that made it illegal for free Africans to own property. New York enacted similar restrictive legislation, as a result of violence in 1712, prohibiting free Africans from owning property, land or houses. Only three Africans or three Natives were allowed to be in a public place at the same time. It would not be until 1809 that New York allowed Africans to marry.

It is probable that Richard Pierpoint was familiar with New York prior to the American Revolution. Whether he had escaped, bought his freedom or was still enslaved at the time of the revolution, he had some connection to the most prominent families in the Mohawk Valley. His commanding officer during the War of Independence was John Butler, the owner of the Butlersbury estate, a judge in Tryon County and the Grand Master of the New York Freemasons.

John Butler was a Justice of the Peace and Lieutenant Colonel of militia while living in Butlersbury, New York. He was also a Freemason and was
named as the Charter Secretary of St. Patrick's
Lodge in 1766.

The Mohawk Valley at the time of the Revolutionary War was a
frontier region. The Hodenausaunee, the League of the Great Peace,
called the Six Nations by the British, was still the dominant power in
the middle Great Lakes and Upper New York region. Their numbers,
however, were much reduced, a result of epidemics of European-intro-
duced diseases. Despite their position of strength, the League had
never been established as a territorial state on the European model,
and later non-native observers have tended to underestimate the influence and power the Six Nations had and still possessed.

The core of the territory of the League was based in the Finger
Lakes region of what is now Upper New York State, but around the
time of first Eurpoean contact, Six Nations' power stretched from the
eastern seaboard west to the Mississippi Valley and south into
Kentucky. This "power" can be seen as a type of loose empire, a

combination trade network and alliance system, based on family connections and the underlying threat of military retaliation.

The society that arose in the Mohawk Valley was a unique multi-ethnic experiment, whose development was to a large degree, arrested by the outbreak of the revolution. As well as the League, there were the long-established Dutch families dating from the time the colony belonged to the Netherlands. There were more recent arrivals from Palatine Germany, mostly religious refugees, and, as well, there were Scots and settlers from New England and Pennsylvania, the second and third generation descendants of the first English settlement families.

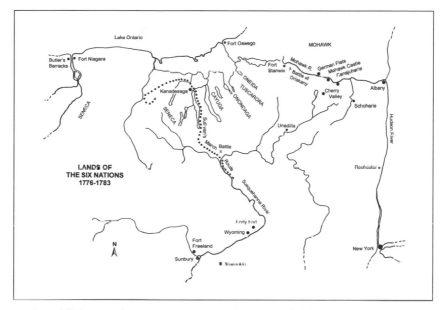

In addition to these, there were a number of Africans, most of them slaves. But there were also free Africans, some having descended from those who had bought their way out of slavery as early as the period of Dutch rule, a hundred years earlier. Many of them spoke Dutch and were members of the Dutch Reformed Church, being third or fourth generation New Yorkers. A number of other Africans had escaped and been adopted into Native communities. Here, Africans were accepted fairly rapidly as Natives did not practise discrimination based on skin colour. At this time, the term "mulatto" tended to refer specifically to people of mixed Indian-African descent, only after the late 1700s did it take on its current meaning of European-African mix.[12]

Sir William Johnson, shown here in his Baronet guise, was just as comfortable dressed as a Mohawk during his time in the region of New York.

In addition to Dutch Reformed, the Europeans and their African servants attended the Church of England and other smaller Protestant sects. It is likely that Africans in the Mohawk Valley maintained some of their native religious practices, even while attending Christian churches. Among the Six Nations, there was also much diversity. Generally the Mohawk are considered the most Christianized, mainly following the Church of England, while the Seneca held mostly to their traditional rituals. The Oneida and Tuscarora had large numbers influenced by New England Protestant missionaries. In additon, there were significant communities of Roman Catholics, many of these stemming from the Wyandot and Neutral peoples adopted into the Six Nations during the wars of the 1640s.

The Mohawk Valley was by no means an idyllic Arcadia. There were tensions between the older established families and the newer arrivals from Connecticut and Pennsylvania. Border disputes between the colonies of New York and New Hampshire in the Vermont region, and with Pennsylvania in the Susquehanna Valley, had already erupted into violence in the past. Religious and political differences would also see the Six Nations split.

The most important man in the area was Sir William Johnson, Superintendent of Indian Affairs for the colonies north of the Ohio River. At the age of twenty-two, this Irishman had moved to the Mohawk Valley in 1737, and started a prosperous trading relationship with the Mohawks. He learned their languages and customs, and would paint his face and dress as they did when among them. In 1760, he received 66,000 acres from the Six Nations because of his close association with them. By the time his first wife died in 1759, Johnson had three children. Later, he married Molly Brant with whom he had eight children. Molly, one of the most influential Mohawks, was invaluable to Sir William when it came to relations with the Six Nations. Her brother, Thayendinagea, known in English as Joseph Brant, became one of the greatest Mohawk war chiefs. He would have been well-known to Richard Pierpoint.

The Deputy Superintendent of Indian Affairs was William Johnson's long time friend John Butler, who later formed Butler's Rangers, the unit in which Pierpoint served as a free man. Butler was born in New London, Connecticut in 1728. His mother, Deborah Dennis, was from a third generation Connecticut family, while his father, Walter, had come to America from Ireland as a subaltern in the British army in 1711. A commander of local militia units for a number of years, he was posted to Fort Hunter on the Mohawk River shortly after John's birth. John Butler was educated in Connecticut, before his father moved the family to the Mohawk Valley where he had acquired a substantial property across the river from Fort Hunter. John was 14 years old at the time. In 1752 he married Catharine Bradt of an old and prominent Dutch family. During his years along the Mohawk he had mastered several Iroquoian languages, enabling him to serve as the chief interpreter under Sir William Johnson during the French-Indian War.

After the war, Butler returned to managing his estate and raising his five children. By this time, he was considered to be the second wealthiest man along the Mohawk, after Johnson. His estate of Butlersbury covered 26,600 acres in the fertile valley.

The lifestyle along the Mohawk was lavish for the Johnsons and Butlers, even though the winds of trouble were starting to stir in the

Johnson Hall was used as a model farm by William Johnson to encourage and train Six Nations men in European farming methods. The slaves who worked on the farm lived in their own accommodations found behind the stone storehouse on the right of Johnson Hall.

British colonies. In 1763, William Johnson had a Georgian house built beside the Cayadutta Creek, about 14 miles north of the Mohawk River. The house contained the best furnishings and the latest books, along with monkeys and parrots, some of the pets making up part of the household. Johnson Hall, as the estate was called, was set up as a model farm to encourage settlement and to demonstrate what could be achieved with a well-run agricultural operation. The bouwmaster or head farmer was an Irishman named Flood. He looked after the 10 to 15 slaves and their families who tended the formal gardens, the crops and the livestock. These slaves who dressed as the Natives did, but wore coats as well, had their own accommodations in cabins across the creek from the main house.

A large staff was required to keep the household running smoothly, all of which was managed by Molly. She was said to dress in the "Indian Manner" although she also wore European style clothing at other times. It is likely that the servants spoke Mohawk as well as English, since Molly would use the native language with the children, her family and Mohawk visitors. Between ten and thirty guests would be at Johnson Hall on most days, as travellers in the area would stop by to pay their respects to Sir William and Molly. After such a visit, Judge Thomas described the daily routine in the house:

"...from all parts of America, from Europe, and from the West Indies...The gentlemen and ladies breakfasted in their respective rooms, and, at their option, had either tea, coffee, or chocolate, or if an old rugged veteran wanted a beef-steak, a mug of ale, a glass of brandy, or some grog, he called for it, and it was always at his service. The freer people made, the more happy was Sir William. After breakfast, while Sir William was about his business, his guests entertained themselves as they pleased. Some rode out, some went out with guns, some with fishing-tackle, some sauntered about the town, some played cards, some backgammon, some billiards, some pennies, and some even at nine-pins. Thus was each day spent until the hour of four, when the bell punctually rang for dinner, and all assembled. He had besides his own family, seldom less than ten, sometimes thirty. All were welcome. All sat down together. All was good cheer, mirth, and festivity. Sometimes seven, eight or ten, of the Indian Sachems joined the festive board. His dinners were plentiful. They consisted, however, of the produce of his estate, or what was procured from the woods and rivers, such as venison, bear, and fish of every kind, with wild turkeys, partridges, grouse, and quails in abundance. No jellies, ragouts, or sillibubs graced his table. His liquors were Madeira, ale, strong beer, cider, and punch. Each guest chose what he liked, and drank as he pleased. The company, or at least a part of them, seldom broke up before three in the morning. Every one, however, Sir William included, retired when he pleased. There was no restraint."[13]

The names of some of the slaves show up in Johnson's papers, usually when they were bought or sold. Only first names were used, such as those of two house servants, Nicholas and Flora. The other slave that can be identified was Pontiac, Sir William's waiter. Pontiac was of mixed African and Native heritage. Cornplanter, one of the two primary war leaders of the Seneca, was the son of a European (possibly Dutch or Scotch), John Abeel, and a Seneca woman. Later in his life, Abeel would only let Natives and "a few Negroes" into his house.[14] Another Seneca was Sun Fish, a free mulatto, who acted as a courier and intelligence gatherer for John Johnson, Sir William's son. At one time, Sir William held a wedding with 18 whites marrying Natives.

This mixing of the cultures of the three continents created an interesting situation in this area of New York, with, generally-speaking, the most powerful men in the northern British colonies respecting the various cultures. Sir William managed to maintain a balance among the diverse peoples living in his sphere of influence until his death. However, the upcoming battles between Patriots and Loyalists eventually led to a civil war that tore apart the societies of both the European settlers of the Mohawk and the Six Nations.

4   The Rhythm of War

The distinctive staccato of the drum beats signified a call for recruits. How many times had Richard Pierpoint heard this call? In his native Bundu and here in British North America, the drum was both a symbol and signal of war. The year was 1777, the third year of conflict between the rebel British colonists and the Loyalist forces. It had been a disastrous year for the forces loyal to King George III, with the defeat of General Burgoyne's army at Saratoga and the loss of the middle Hudson and Mohawk river valleys. Still, the British maintained control of the forts at Niagara and Oswego, and from here they could provide support, both material and moral, to their Six Nations allies , who dominated the headwaters of the Mohawk and Susquehanna rivers. Further American advances towards the Great Lakes would not prove easy.

Native war parties had surprising mobility for those used to European massed armies, dependent on prepared magazines with food, fodder and ammunition. Able to live off the land, sleep in the open and cover long distances by canoe on the extensive river systems of the east coast and Midwest, even a small military force of the Iroquois League (or Six Nations; they called themselves Hodenausaunee) could inflict punishing damage on an uncooperative village.

Only a few Europeans understood that the vast distances and rugged terrain of the hinterland of the North American east coast could not be controlled by what would be considered normal methods in the Old World. In terms of military strategy, a medium-sized European army of 50,000 men would simply be swallowed up in what was called the "wilderness." Indeed, no such concentration of force was possible, and, at that time in North America a regular army of 8000 was considered huge. But those who understood the American environment did not see it as desert. To the contrary, forces of

100 to 500 men could survive for months by combining easily portable provisions, supplemented by foraging, with backup provided by a network of friendly villages and settlements, and still be capable of rapid movement. Such forces, as the League of the Hodenausaunee had shown, could control a huge territory with only a limited number of fighting men involved.

The few men who understood this included Robert Rogers, William Johnson and John Butler. In fact, the successful performance of Butler's small unit of Rangers and its Native allies at the Battle of Oriskany, during the siege of Fort Stanwix, was one of the few positive points for the Loyalists in 1777. Here, a mixed Native-British force, including Butler's volunteers, ambushed a rebel relief column and virtually annihilated it. Butler's force of irregulars was modelled on Rogers' Rangers, a unit that made a name for itself, devastating Abenaki villages in Quebec during the previous Seven Years War. Made up of settlers from New England, the unit had been organized and trained to fight in the irregular warfare methods of the Six Nations. The emphasis was on hit-and-run raids, ambushes and rapid mobility through dense forest and rough terrain. Rogers codified his ideas in 28 points which covered operations in small numbers or larger groups of up to 300 or 400. To avoid being surprised by enemy forces, discipline was key, both during the march and when making camp.

The strategic goal was to distract regular enemy forces, while the burning of crops and dwellings would cause economic devastation, thus undercutting the logistical base of enemy military operations. These attacks also sought to directly undermine the morale of both civilians and soldiers. With their home and families open to attack, militia forces, although usually vastly superior in numbers, were reluctant to move far afield from their own communities. This made tracking and catching the highly mobile Ranger strike forces difficult. In modern terminology, such methods would be called guerrilla warfare and terrorism. The influence small Ranger companies exerted along the frontier was far out of proportion to the number of men involved.

Butler's Rangers came to reflect all of the cultural complexities of the Mohawk Valley. Butler himself came from an Anglo-Irish background. Recruits represented families from diverse origins, such as the Scottish McDonell's, the Dutch Ten Broeck's or the Servos family from Central Europe. Eventually, the unit also came to include West Africans like Pierpoint. On September 15, 1777, the

Fort Niagara had been constructed by the French to control the fur trade through the Great Lakes. John Butler was part of the British force that had taken it from the French in 1759. Richard Pierpoint would see service in the fort during the American Revolution and the War of 1812.

British commander, Sir Guy Carleton, issued a "beating order" authorizing Butler to establish a permanent corps of rangers:

> "By virtue of the power in me vested by the King, I do hereby authorize and empower you, or such officers as you shall direct, by Beat of Drum or otherwise, forthwith to raise on the frontiers of the Province, so many able bodied men of His Majesty's loyal subjects as will form one company of Rangers, to serve with the Indians as occasion shall require."[1]

The order set the size of the company at 50 privates, six non-commissioned officers and two lieutenants and a captain. Butler was soon given further permission to raise an additional seven companies after the first was completely mustered and equipped ready for service, to form a full battalion of eight companies.

With the loss of the Mohawk Valley to the American Patriots, the Rangers were to be based at Fort Niagara, which was also the garrison of the 8th Foot, a regular British army regiment, plus units of engineers and artillery. Detachments of the 8th at times participated in

Ranger raids as well. At first the new recruits were housed in any storage buildings not in use, but in 1778, Butler began the construction of a real barracks near the fort on the west side of the Niagara River. Few, if any, in the spring of 1778 realized they would never go back to their beloved Mohawk Valley again, and that the simple barracks would become the foundation of their new home, a settlement that would eventually grow into the town of Niagara-on-the-Lake.

But that still lay some years in the future. The initial recruits included many of those who had fought at Oriskany under Butler, or had been employees of the Indian Department. This body functioned as a kind of combination embassy-foreign office for the various Native nations along the St. Lawrence Valley and Great Lakes. The Department (later divided into eastern and western sections), which maintained its own small military forces independent of the regular army, in the Great Lakes area had the primary goal of keeping the Iroquois and Shawnee allied to the Crown. By mid-December, the mustering of the company was complete. Service with the Rangers was made attractive as it paid 4 shillings per day (rates varied during the war) for a private, well above the regular army pay rates. Additional recruits were sought at every opportunity.

Indeed, one key task during any operation was to find new recruits. The remote settlements along the frontiers of Pennsylvania, New Jersey and New York were the most important target zones. Recruiting parties might be out for months at a time. Often they would be based at a native village and, once a suitable number of Loyalists was gathered, the group would head back to Fort Niagara. This task was full of danger, as the small groups of partly armed, untrained recruits were vulnerable to capture by enemy patrols. The whole group might be treated as spies and traitors and be subject to execution.

Service as a ranger was no easy task, however. Carleton's order stipulated that of the eight companies, two were to be composed of people speaking one or more native languages, and be "acquainted with their customs and manner of making war."[2] These two companies were seen as a form of elite, which would be working closely with the League and their allies. As for the remaining companies, recruits had to be "people well acquainted with the woods ... in consideration of the fatigues they are liable to undergo."[3]

On May 2, 1778 there were three full ranger companies. One company under Captain Barent Frey made a separate raid in Pennsylvania, while Butler himself and Captain William Caldwell took 200 Rangers and 300 Indians on an expedition to Wyoming (present day Wilkes-Barre, Pennsylvania). All the actions were successful, with Butler defeating the garrison of Forty Fort, the most important military post at Wyoming, after luring the Americans into an ambush.

The most punishing raid led by Butler's Rangers, however, came in November against Cherry Valley. The garrison of the town, caught by surprise, fled to the nearby fort leaving the civilians to fend for themselves. It proved to be a disastrous decision. A number of residents fired in self defence. Once the residents of Cherry Valley offered resistance, the whole community was exposed to danger. A number of Seneca, led by Little Beard, began to wreak a terrible revenge, slaughtering men, women and children. This group of Seneca had been enraged by the boast of an American commander named Hartley claiming that he would kill any Native he found. Other Natives, however, refused to participate in the killing and looting, and some actively protected the unarmed settlers. Some settlers survived by being taken as prisoners. These could be ransomed later or adopted into the Native community to replace previous losses. Individuals who were known to have treated the Natives fairly were spared. In many cases, the opposing individuals, often enough related by blood or marriage, knew each other at least by name if not by face. Altogether 33 civilians were killed and about 70 taken prisoner during the bloody battle.

The crop and property damage inflicted by the Rangers to the rich farmlands along the Susquehanna and Hudson valleys was affecting supplies to General George Washington's Continental army. In the community of German Flats along the Mohawk, five mills and 120 buildings were destroyed, and 826 cattle described as taken. In the Wyoming Valley, "the river and the roads down it were it covered with men, women and children fleeing for their lives..."[4] In 1780, raids over three days in and around Schoharie resulted in the destruction of 13 mills, 1000 houses and 600,000 bushels of grain. "The settlement of Schoharie alone would have delivered 80,000 bushels of grain [to the Continental army], but that fine district is now totally destroyed," lamented one letter to General Washington.[5]

The battle at Cherry Valley cemented John Butler's reputation as a blood-thirsty demon in the American colonies. Cherry Valley became a rallying cry for the Patriots, and vengeance was demanded. The solution to the Ranger problem was Sullivan's raid of 1779.

General Washington gave Major-General John Sullivan the task of eliminating the Iroquois threat once and for all. Seemingly, the Americans tended to neglect the importance of the Rangers and, instead, focused their effort against the Six Nations, although the ultimate goal of the campaign was the capture of Fort Niagara. Sullivan massed a force of 670 officers and 4445 other ranks at Tioga on the Pennsylvania frontier. Butler had only 270 rangers, 14 regulars from the 8th Foot, Brant's Volunteer's (30 whites and natives), 30 Delawares and about 300 Seneca under Sangerachta. Still an imposing and robust figure at more than 70 years old and standing more than 6' tall, he was the League's most respected war hero.

Sullivan had his own problems, however. The Continental commissariat, responsible for financing the American war effort, was chronically underfunded and the purchasing Sullivan's supplies, with beef, flour and liquor as the staples, was slower than expected. Even when provisions were stockpiled, it was difficult to move them. The army had to resort to requisitioning wagons, teams and drivers from local farmers who were reluctant to hire out their carts for even relatively generous wages (40 dollars a month).[6] It was well known that wagons and draft horses lent to the army had a tendency to come back in none-too-good repair, if they came back at all. Sullivan's campaign was severely delayed and Washington's scorched earth strategy ultimately failed to break the resistance of the League and the Rangers, although heavy damage was done to Iroquois settlements and farms. The war dragged on.

Both the Loyalists and the Patriots had been reluctant to arm large numbers of Indians and slaves, for obvious reasons. A large group of armed and trained slaves would unlikely be willing to return to their servile state once the war was finished, which ever side won. Nor was either side keen to encourage Native resistance, which could easily develop into a general anti-European conflict. (Pontiac's Shawnee coalition of western nations in 1763 was an all too recent reminder of what such a native alliance could do.)[7]

However, as the war dragged on, and as the military situation for the Loyalists worsened, the British especially felt pressure to seek allies where ever they might be found. After Sullivan's 1779 campaign, mass Native participation was encouraged, both in the Hudson and Susquehanna valleys and to the south and west of Detroit.

Recruiting slaves remained more problematic. Loyalists were as reluctant as the Patriots to give up their property, risking loss of their

An African member of Butler's Rangers would have dressed in typical campaign gear which included a green hunting jacket, buckskin breeches and the black cap with a brass frontplate. Some Rangers fortified their caps with iron bands to help deflect blows to the head.

slaves through battle or desertion. However, a small number of servants did follow their owners into the army. Where African slaves were taken into British service, most were used in labour or transportation units. Examples of these are the Royal Bateauxmen, raised in Jamaica, or the Black Company of Pioneers, raised in Philadelphia in late 1777. Relatively few were used in combat units, although the East Florida Rangers in June 1779 had 150 Africans out of 860 troops and the Jamaica Rangers, with 474 men, was all Black. This unit, however, served only in the West Indies.

The more effective recruitment strategy, however, was encouraging slaves owned by rebels to desert, with the offer of freedom in exchange of service in the Loyalist forces. This not only gained needed recruits, but it also undercut the enemy economy. One of the first successful units was a Virginia militia battalion, Dunmore's Ethiopians. In November 1775, Lord John Dunmore, the Royal Governor of Virginia, offered freedom to rebel-owned slaves who joined the forces loyal to the Crown. More than 300 Africans responded. A general offer of freedom in exchange for military duty only came almost four years later, on July 3, 1779. The numbers of African slaves who took up the offer are not known with certainty.

Richard Pierpoint enters the historical record in 1780, listed as one of Butler's Rangers at Fort Niagara. The records also show that he was receiving food for a woman while stationed there.[8] There is no indication of who she was. As slaves of Loyalists were not generally freed, it is likely Pierpoint was a run-away. From the available documents there are less than a dozen known Africans who served in Butler's Rangers. Two of these, the brothers Peter and Richard Martin, were the slaves of John Butler (while Peter Martin's son was a slave of Thomas Butler). They had been captured by rebels and resold, but then managed to escape and rejoin Butler.

While no official record has been found of Pierpoint from his arrival in America in 1760 to his reappearance in Niagara 20 years later, an advertisement for a suspected runaway slave by the name Richard Pierpoint, appears in the 1779 March 13 and 23 editions of the *Pennsylvania Packet and Daily Advertiser*. The notice reads:

"Sunbury, Northumberland County, March 4. Was committed to my custody the 23 of October last, on suspicion of designing to go to the enemy, or being runaway slaves, two Negro Men; one named James Hays, say he drove a team in the Continental service for William Stull, living at the Head of Elk; the other named Richard Pierpoint, says he also drove a team in the Continental service for Henry Stull, of the same place... Richard Pierpoint is about twenty-six years of age, about five feet three or four inches high, has very large eyes and thick lips, seems fond of strong liquor, but is very civil and bidable. The above described Negroes say that they, with their waggons, were taken by the enemy at Rhode Island, and carried to between White Plains and New-York, from whence they made their escape, and on their return missed their road, and wandered about until they struck on the N.E. branch of the river Susquehanna, above Shamokin, where they were taken up. They both say they are free, and were discharged by Proclamation at the last Court of General Quarter Sessions of the Peace held for the county aforesaid, on the 23d of February last, from the impeachment of their intention of going to the enemy, no witnesses appearing against them; they are therefore now confined on no other accusation than a suspicion of being runaway slaves. Their master or masters, if any they have, are desired to come prove their property, pay charges and take them away in six weeks from the date hereof, otherwise they will be sold out for their fees by George Keiser, Gaoler."

However, a subsequent notice which appeared in Benjamin Franklin's *Pennsylvania Gazette* of January 19, 1780, shows that Pierpoint was still in custody. This advertisement, dated December 19, 1779, Sunbury, calls the prisoner Richard Lincoln "formerly advertised by the name of Pierpoint."[10] The same physical description is given, but with the added detail that Pierpoint/Lincoln "seems to have been bred a barber."[11] The notice also adds that both Hays and Pierpoint allegedly belonged to a Mr. Dorsey of Frederick, Maryland. Was Pierpoint a false name, or Lincoln? And if Pierpoint was an alias, where did Richard Lincoln get this name? Had he met another slave called Pierpoint? Or did the authorities have information that a certain Dorsey of Maryland was missing a slave called Richard Lincoln, and that possibly the man they had in custody was this person using a false name? Any of these suppositions are possible. The jailer, in this case a John Morrison, again states that both men will be "sold out as the law directs"[12] if no one came forth to claim them after six weeks. That could mean months or years of servitude to pay the costs of their advertising and maintenance while in jail.

For the Richard Pierpoint of Bundu the age is incorrect, as he would have been 34 years of age in 1778. But the age in the notice is clearly a guess, "about 26," and an underestimate is not impossible, the physical differences between a 26 and 34 year old would not necessarily be noticeable. It was also not uncommon for runaway slaves to provide

> Sunbury, Northumberland County, March 4.
> WAS committed to my custody the 23d of October last, on suspicion of designing to go to the enemy, or being runaway slaves, two Negro Men; one named JAMES HAYS, says he drove a team in the Continental service for William Stull, living at the Head of Elk; the other named RICHARD PIERPOINT, says he also drove a team in the Continental service for Henry Stull, of the same place. James Hays is a likely intelligent fellow, about five feet ten inches high, twenty three years of age or thereabouts, is sober and mannerly. Richard Pierpoint is about twenty-six years of age, about five feet three or four inches high, has large eyes and thick lips, seems fond of strong liquor, but is very civil and bidable. The above described Negroes say that they, with their waggons, were taken by the enemy at Rhode Island, and carried to between White Plains and New-York, from whence they made their escape, and on their return missed their road, and wandered about until they struck on the N. E. branch of the river Susquehanna, above Shamokin, where they were taken up. They both say they are free, and were discharged by Proclamation at the last Court of General Quarter Sessions of the Peace held for the county aforesaid, on the 23d of February last, from the impeachment of their intentions of going to the enemy, no witnesses appearing against them; they are therefore now confined on no other accusation than a suspicion of being run-away slaves. Their master or masters, if any they have, are desired to come, prove their property, pay charges and take them away in six weeks from the date hereof, otherwise they will be sold out for their fees, by
> GEORGE KEISER, Gaoler.

The first mention of Richard Pierpoint came in this 1779 advertisement. It was printed in the *Pennsylvania Packet and Daily Advertiser* which was published by John Dunlap, a trusted friend of George Washington.

misleading information to make their return to their owners more difficult. One duty of an officer's servant was barbering, so this was certainly a skill Pierpoint could have learned.

A relatively large battle was fought in Rhode Island, on August 29, 1778, between the British garrison of Newport and an American besieging force under John Sullivan. The port, the one major base the British maintained in New England, was the target of a combined Franco-American offensive. However, the attack was abandoned after the French fleet was forced to withdraw to Boston on August 20 to repair damage suffered in a severe storm. Sullivan watched some 3000

The stone walls of the Sunbury jail make up the foundation for this building in the Pennsylvania town. Situated
on the town square, the prisoners in the jail were in close
proximity to the whipping post across the street. Lashing
was a common punishment in colonial Pennsylvania.

militia desert after the French left, and before he could withdraw his
own weakened army, the British garrison struck. It was a hotly
contested fight, but one conducted mostly at long musket range. There
was little close-in fighting and casualties were limited. The Americans
listed 44 missing, a total that would include any prisoners.

Some 200 Africans had recently enlisted in the rebel 1st Rhode
Island Regiment. Desperate for recruits, the colony's government had

offered freedom for any slave willing to fight, but the expected response proved to be disappointing, and the offer was withdrawn on June 10. The 1st Rhode Island was among one of the most heavily engaged units during the battle, but Pierpoint's story, that both he and his wagon were captured, shows he was still with the transport services (indeed, it was more typical to find enlisted men being taken out of the line to be used as teamsters, rather than the reverse). Both Hays and Pierpoint maintained they were freemen, perhaps believing the offer of freedom also extended to men employed in the transport corps—although many apprehended slaves made this claim.

The chances of Pierpoint being captured during the battle were extremely remote, considering there had been neither a rout nor a breakthrough by the British into the American rear areas. Raids by the British fleet along the coast did occur, and Hays and Pierpoint could have been captured here. However, it is also possible the whole story of capture was concocted and that both men were among the thousands of deserters that left Sullivan after August 20. In any case, Pierpoint and Hays did not seem anxious to regain American lines. Major American bases were located not far upstream on the Hudson, or if these were blocked by British patrols, the two could have headed towards New Jersey and Philadelphia. But the two were arrested far along the Susquehanna Valley near the small settlement of Shamokin—after more than a month of wandering in the sparsely settled and heavily forested Appalachians. Free or not, Africans travelling on their own without any form of papers indicating their status were liable for arrest. Certainly, the authorities did not believe the story and accused the two of attempting to escape to the British. Lacking witnesses, these charges were dropped in February, but the men were then held as escaped slaves. It has, so far, not been possible to find out what happened to Richard Pierpoint/Lincoln, after the six weeks deadline. However, the whole story does provide some possible scenarios, and inherent difficulties, of how a slave could have ended up with the British forces.

What we can say is that in the late winter and early spring there was a person by the name of Richard Pierpoint, of uncertain legal standing and background, right on the frontier of war where Butler's Rangers were most active. Sunbury was on the main route north along the Susquehanna Valley, then a village of 100 buildings, a busy commercial centre on the edge of white settlement and the site of Fort Augusta. The Wyoming Valley, the scene of repeated ranger raids, was about 50 kilometres, a two- or three-day march upstream, along the main branch of the Susquehanna. In July 1779, Captain John McDonell's company of Butler's Rangers had raided Fort Freeland, only a day's march from Sunbury. He had planned to attack the village then, but his Seneca allies wished to return home with the herd of cattle already taken. Likewise, in the summer of 1780, ranger units were again active within a day's march of the settlement. Almost one hundred men had been recruited by one ranger officer operating among the frontier settlements of the Susquehanna. With the devastation and depopulation caused by the war, labour was in high demand. It is possible that Pierpoint, hired out to a local farmer to repay his costs of maintenance, was captured or ran off during one of these raids. Either as an escaped slave, or as a free man sold back into slavery, Pierpoint now had a clear motive for joining the British following the emancipation offer of the summer of 1779.

It was unusual enough for an African to serve in a combat unit, but it was especially noteworthy that Pierpoint should end up in such a specialized unit as Butler's Rangers. He must have had some knowledge of Indian languages or skills as a woodsman, for certainly the Pierpoint/Lincoln of the newspaper notice had survived more than a month of wandering. Perhaps, he had the physical stamina and enthusiasm to serve as a ranger. In 1780, those were the kind of men Butler needed. After the Sullivan campaign, Butler needed men to build up his numbers. Two of the largest groups recruited that year were 45 men from New Jersey, gathered by Lieutenant Andrew Bradt, and 59 men from the Mohawk Valley brought by Lieutenant Peter Ball and Second Lieutenant Joseph Ferris. But smaller numbers of Loyalists arrived all the time, often with their families. Most noncombatants were sent to Montreal or Machiche, but numbers of women and children remained at the fort.

In the spring of 1780, Butler had eight full strength companies, forming a complete battalion. In the winter of 1780-81, he was authorized to raised ninth and tenth companies. One company was usually based at Detroit, the remainder operated from Niagara. Muster Rolls for Butler's unit are incomplete, but considering Pierpoint's later association with Captains Benjamin Pawling and Peter Ten Broeck, he may have served in one of their companies.

Sullivan's campaign of the summer and fall of 1779 had won the Americans less than six months respite from raids. With the loss of so

Pierpoint may have been held in Fort Augusta when first captured in order to determine his status. The fort was located on this site along the Susquehanna River in Sunbury. The marker commemorates "Sullivan's Expedition Against the Iroquois Indians, 1779", the same year the name Richard Pierpoint was advertised as a fugitive slave.

many Native villages as forward bases, and with many of the American farms between the Mohawk and Susquehanna likewise devastated, the Rangers had to move over ever longer distances. Still, in spite of the severe cold that winter, Butler's men, including Pierpoint, were active by February and ready to strike the New York and Pennsylvania frontiers in April. The most devastating raids were made in August, with the Mohawk Valley to the east and the Wyoming Valley

The Treaty of Paris divided the falls at Niagara between Britain and the United States. This 1796 view shows the American Falls on the left and the Horseshoe Falls on the right. The Niagara River became a popular crossing point for escaping American slaves.

to the south again taking the brunt. Towards the Ohio Valley, the Detroit Ranger company had forced the Americans to retreat back to Fort Pitt.

In the following year, raiders struck as far as Bedford Township, deep in Pennsylvania on the border of Maryland. Other Rangers burned a settlement in Rochester (Township) along the Hudson, 18 kilometres from the rebel capital of Kingston, New York, some 400 kilometres from Niagara. In 1782, a mounted force under the legendary American frontiersman, Daniel Boone, was ambushed and scattered on August 18 by a mixed Native-Ranger force under Captain Caldwell at Blue Licks, while another force under Captain Andrew Bradt burned Wheeling, West Virginia.

Butler's Rangers and their brother units remained active until the end of the war. Although the Treaty of Paris, ending the war between the British and what was now the new nation of the United States of America, was signed in 1783, the last unit of Butler's Rangers was not disbanded until the spring of 1784. It was largely through the efforts of the Rangers and their native allies that the British had retained any hold on the Great Lakes region.

To the dismay of Butler and his Loyalist followers, the Mohawk and Hudson valleys and the League homelands were given up by Britain and assigned to the Americans. With thousands of now homeless people in residence, Niagara was transformed from a military base into a frontier town. The process had already been underway for a number of years. Many soldiers' families had taken up residence at the fort as their homesteads had been destroyed or occupied by the Patriots. As well, farms had been opened up around the fort to provide supplemental food for the garrison. The League of the Hodenausaunee was split. Some members stayed within the new United States, but the remainder were granted land along the Grand River by the Mississauga Ojibwa, in a deal brokered by the Indian Department. Niagara, for many people a symbol of their exile, for Richard Pierpoint represented his first home as a free man since his capture and removal from Bundu almost 25 years before.

5   A Man of Colour

Thousands of war-weary refugees crowded around the British strong-hold of Fort Niagara as the Treaty of Paris ended the American Revolution in 1783. Farming had started around the fort during the war, both to support the troops and to feed the refugees. Across the Niagara River, the construction of barracks initiated by John Butler in 1778, were set within flooding distance of a marsh. Butler's Barracks become the nucleus for a small settlement.

By 1781, four or five families, including the Butlers, had built houses near the barracks. This cluster of buildings became the first permanent English-speaking settlement in southern Ontario, and quickly grew into a town known as Niagara.[1] Among the linden trees, old elms and weeping willows, a gridwork of roads was laid out in the typical British square pattern. Houses started to appear along the wide streets. The sixteen families that showed up on a 1782 census grew to 45 families by the following year.[2]

Africans were an integral part of the frontier town's life. In 1783, Governor Sir Frederick Haldimand requested a census of slaves brought into Canada with Loyalist forces. Six names appeared from Niagara, one was listed as "Dick (Colonel John Butler, former master)."[3] This would have been Richard Martin who had been a member of Butler's Rangers. The Butler household had more slaves, but they did not end up on the census. This shows that there were more African residents in the town at its beginnings.

The location of the town of Niagara was possible because the land had been acquired in a treaty with the Seneca made by Sir William Johnson in 1764. The deal, which encompassed a depth of four miles and a length of fourteen miles on each side of the river, had also been agreed to by the Ojibwa. However, this amount of land would only accommodate a small portion of the refugees who had made their way north from the former British colonies. The rest of the Loyalists, with no hope of ever returning home, were in a desperate situation. The colonial leaders, knowing that they had to act quickly, forged an agreement with the Ojibwa to acquire more land along the shores of Lake Ontario.

Surveyors were chosen to begin the task of dividing the lush hardwood forests and fertile meadows into rectangular lots. The men chosen to do the job did not always have a solid background in the craft of surveying, but they managed divide up the land into roughly rectangular lots that were roughly 100 acres in size.

The government had decided that officers and soldiers would receive grants for property of varying sizes depending upon their rank. A system was also set up to take care of the area's homeless residents. A list was developed identifying the United Empire Loyalists, as they became known, who would receive at least a 100 acre land grant for remaining loyal to the crown. The British governor, Sir Frederick Haldimand, had suggested that deserving blacks should receive 50 acres. Sir John Johnson, who was in charge of the land grants for the Kingston area, disagreed and argued that he thought the blacks should receive the same proportion of land as other men. However, he suggested that these grants should go to the owner, not the slave himself. This, of course, would mean a substantial increase of land for slave-owners like Johnson, with no benefit for the hapless slaves. Ultimately, it seems to have been left up to local government officials as to which free African settlers were to receive land. Slaves received nothing.

Of the thousands of names on the Loyalist list only a handful were those of black men. It is estimated that the population of Upper Canada in the 1780s was between 10 and 14 thousand. The number of Africans included in this amount has always been considered to be small, usually only 5% or about 500 people. However, in 1778 there were already 127 blacks at Detroit and, by 1791 there were 300 slaves in the Niagara area.[4] Sir John Johnson had brought back 30 blacks from the Mohawk Valley after a raid in 1780. Seventeen were the property of just three well-to-do men, including Johnson who later made a claim for compensation for 11 slaves that were left behind. There were also African slaves in the Loyalist settlements along Lake Ontario near present day Kingston. Four families, including that of Major Peter van Alstine, had at least ten slaves each. Prominent social and political figures such as Peter Russell, William Jarvis, James and Robert Isaac Dey Gray and Peter Robinson had many slaves. Russell was said to have had ninety-nine.[5]

The west end of the province also had its share of slaveowners. Matthew Elliott, a wealthy landowner and former army officer, accumulated 3,000 acres around Amherstburg. His estate was kept running by the labour of up to 60 slaves, both African and Native. But slaves were not just the property of the upper class in British North America. An African slave would have been no more uncommon a household possession than a dishwasher is today. In 1790, the British government encouraged immigration into any British territory with legislation that allowed United States residents to import "...negros, household furniture, utensils of husbandry or cloathing, duty free."[6]

It is likely that the African slave population was close to one thousand in Upper Canada by 1793. At the start of American Revolution there were half a million African slaves in British North America, about 20% of the population.[7]

The number of free Africans living in Upper Canada is even more difficult to determine than the slave population. We do know that the British government paid 500,000 pounds (about 5,000 people at £100 per slave) to the state of Virginia as compensation for the African slaves who had escaped to the British during the war.[8] A number of these slaves, as well as free Africans made their way to the province. However, unless an African had fought as a free man during the war, he did not receive a land grant in Upper Canada as his European compatriots did. This deliberate omission led to African settlers moving onto the unsurveyed land that still belonged to the Mississauga Ojibwa.

In these lands, the Africans, many of whom were fugitives from slavery, could find a safe haven from slave catchers and bounty hunters. They also managed to avoid the assessors and census takers which meant that their numbers were never included in official population figures.

It was a common practice for Africans who had escaped from slavery to live with Natives, and Native societies routinely adopted Africans into their villages. Various officials of the British colonies realized this early on and tried to stem such actions. In 1726, the governor of New York asked that the Six Nations Confederacy return African fugitives and, in 1746, the same was asked of the Hurons. A resident of Detroit wrote during the Pontiac rebellion that "The Indians are saving and caressing all the Negroes they take."[9] In 1775, slaves in Ulster County, New York organized an uprising that included 500 Natives. The Natives never returned any fugitive slaves, even though the number which had escaped was huge. Thomas Jefferson estimated that by 1778 about 30,000 slaves ran away in Virginia alone.[10]

As long as these newly-arrived settlers respected the Ojibwa's hunting, fishing and farming territories, the two groups could live in harmony. The Ojibwa were nomadic and would travel across the territory, moving from one area to the next as the seasons changed.

The Africans who managed to make it to Upper Canada did not always find things easy. Many were skilled craftsmen and could provide a valuable service. However, they were not always given the opportunity and, when they were, their wages were often half of that paid to a white person.

This prejudice against Canada's African settlers meant that many people thought of them as worthless and lazy, generally inferior. Richard Pierpoint was one of the Africans in the Niagara area who knew that this perception needed to change. Most of them were first or second generation arrivals from Africa. They had a solid understanding of their history and culture. They knew that they were hardworking, intelligent and decent people. Their African cultures and religions were as ancient and developed as that of their European neighbours and, as well, they had brought valuable skills with them. All they needed was the opportunity to show it. But, it would be difficult for this to happen since land was only given to those who had fought during the war, and the lucky ones who had received land grants were spread throughout the vast province. In eastern Ontario, seven lots in present day Glengarry County went to Cato Prime, James Fonda, Jack Powell, Joseph Goff, William Thomas, Londonderry and Sambo.[11] At the other end of the province, James Robertson received land near Detroit while Joseph Frey's lot was in Essex County.[12] Both had been Butler's Rangers. Pierpoint, meanwhile, had received a grant for land in the Niagara area.

Pierpoint was among a group of free black men who were trying to change their situation in this developing society. They must have held a series of meetings in the spring of 1794. We can only imagine the scene of this large group of African Canadians discussing the problems that their community was facing. The previous year Simcoe's bill banning the importation of slaves had been passed, but those still in slavery remained so. The Chloe Cooley incident was still fresh in their minds. Chloe, a girl owned by William Vrooman, was bound with ropes, dumped into a boat and taken screaming across the Niagara

The statue of Lieutenant-Governor John Graves Simcoe looks over the lawns of Queen's Park, site of Ontario's Legislative Buildings in Toronto. Simcoe was instrumental in planning the development of the new province of Upper Canada.

River. There she was sold to an American, never to be seen again.[13] Another problem they faced was the lack of land since grants were denied to African settlers. Prejudice and discrimination were evident in their working lives as well. The meetings led to a resolution that could be presented to the government. On June 29, 1794, nineteen African men from the Niagara region petitioned Lieutenant Governor John Graves Simcoe. Their petition read:

"That there are a number of Negroes in this part of the Country many of whom have been Soldiers during the late war between

Great Britain & America, and others who were born free with a few who have come into Canada since the peace, - Your Petitioners are desirous of settling adjacent to each other that they may be enabled to give assistance (in work) to those amongst them who may most want it,

Your Petitioners therfore humbly Pray that their situation may be taken into consideration, and if your Excellency should see fit to allow them a Tract of Country to settle on, separate from the white Settlers, your Petitioners hope their behaviour will be such as to shew, that Negroes are capable of being industrious, and in loyalty to the Crown they are not deficient."[14]

The names listed on the petition were: Robert Spranklin, John Gerof, Peter Ling, Jack Baker, Richard Pierpont, Pompadour, Jack Becker, John Cesar, John Jackson, Tom Frey, Jack Wurmwood, John Smith, Peter Green, Michael Grote, Adam Lewis, John Dimon, Simon Speck, Thomas Walker and Saison Sepyed.

Simcoe turned down the petitioners request. It is not known why. Perhaps Simcoe didn't believe that there was a need for the blacks settlers to prove themselves. After all, he had introduced the bill to abolish slavery in Upper Canada. He also must have realized, however, that many citizens of the province saw Africans as subservient. His act of 1793 to end slavery was considerably watered down, the final version of the act allowing slavery to continue in Upper Canada. Anyone who was a slave remained so, while the children of women slaves would remain property for 25 years. There had been very strong opposition to abolishing slavery, and Simcoe may not have wanted to cause further consternation among the province's slaveowners by creating a black enclave that could arbour their runaway slaves.

While the petition was being drafted, Pierpoint was living on his new property. He had received a land board certificate for lots 13 and 14 on the sixth concession in Grantham Township on January 18, 1791, as Richard Parepoint, a pioneer in Butler's Rangers who lived in the Home District.[15] His last name was misspelled, which was not unusual.

Since there were hundreds of African immigrants without land, Richard Pierpoint is likely to have had help in preparing his land for farming. Pierpoint was a well-known figure in the area with years of military service and, with connections to the African, Native and Euro-

Pierpoint's land in Grantham Township sits in the centre of present day St. Catharines, Ontario. St. Catharines would later be home to Harriett Tubman who led many slaves to freedom in Canada.

pean communities, he was an integral part of the Niagara area.

Pierpoint's grant was for 200 acres, an interesting grant since privates were to receive only 100 acres. There are a few possibilities that would have led to Pierpoint being entitled to 200 acres. He could have been considered by his commander, John Butler, to have been a non-commissioned officer; these officers were allotted 200 acres. Or he may have received an extra 100 acres for his inclusion as a United Empire Loyalist. The other possibility is that Captain Dick had family with him when he established himself in Niagara. A soldier was entitled to an additional 50 acres for each family member, and the 1786 victualling records indicated that there was a woman with him. Unfortunately, Pierpoint never appeared on any assessment or census record so it is impossible to tell what his family situation may have been.

In any case, Pierpoint received two 100 acre lots in the middle of Grantham Township. The steep slopes of his land below the Niagara escarpment was touched by a waterway that flowed into Twelve Mile

Dick's Creek was a tributary of Twelve Mile Creek which enters Lake Ontario at Port Dalhousie. This view of Twelve Mile Creek is in the area where Laura Secord was said to have crossed on her way to warn the British troops during the War of 1812.

Butler's Ranger, Daniel Servos owned the first grist mill in the Niagara area. One of his slaves was Robert Jupiter who later served with Pierpoint in the War of 1812. Interestingly, Humphrey Waters, a black recipient of land in the town of Niagara in 1795, named one of his sons Daniel Servos Waters.

Creek, which in turn, emptied into Lake Ontario. In time, settlers came to call this waterway Dick's Creek, an indication that Pierpoint had some status in the area and was well-respected in the community.

It is estimated that five acres of cleared land would sustain a family. So, it is likely that with 200 acres available for use, that other settlers would have worked to clear the land. Loyalists were to receive a set of equipment including axes and farming supplies from the government. Whether Pierpoint received anything is not known. Jacob Dittrick, a sergeant in Butler's Rangers, also received land in Grantham Township. His son, James, described their early settlement experiences:

> "The whole country was forrest, a wilderness that had to be subdued by axe and toil. For a time we had a regular Robinson Cruso life with a few poles and brushwood, formed our tents on the Indian plan. As the clearances enlarged, we were supplied with some agricultural implements, for we brought nothing with us but a few seeds."[16]

Neighbours usually held logging bees to start the farming process. The trees would be felled and trimmed, then be dragged away and burned. The stumps would be left in the ground to rot away, while the crops were planted among them. Some of the seeds provided to the Loyalists were: onions, turnips, cabbage, carrots and peas. Often some tree trunks would be lain end-to-end to form a rough enclosure for the settlers livestock, usually a cow and pigs. The animals would forage among the stumps and in the remaining forest. The cabins were constructed of logs, with a roof made of basswood bark. An open fire-place would be built along one wall. Not luxurious accommodation, but it would keep most of the wind, rain and snow out most of the time. Unfortunately, a lot of the smoke from the fireplace would stay inside, not a very healthy situation. Pierpoint is likely to have lived in such a dwelling for the next fifteen years.

Pierpoint's home was close to the Native trails that traversed the entire area. One of the major routes, known as the Iroquois Trail, ran along the crest of the hill that ran beside Dick's Creek. In 1798, this trail was 30 feet wide, but full of tree stumps. At the point where it crossed Twelve Mile Creek, a wooden bridge was constructed and a settlement called The Twelve developed. The first church in the area was built, sometime before 1796, near Pierpoints' property. From an assignment document dated February 17, 1796, "...to the church at St. Catharines..." comes the suggestion that this Anglican church gave its name to the city of St. Catharines, which ultimately grew up around the settlement.[17] The Iroquois Trail became St. Paul Street, while Dick's Creek became part of the first Welland Canal.

Captain Dick's land must have been a hub of activity, with the value of property rising as commerce grew along the waterways and trade routes. The area's first store, mill and church were close by. As well, the combination of the Native trails that skirted his property and the area's only bridge just downstream must have attracted many of the travellers in the area. Some of these would have been freedom seekers from the United States.

Pierpoint, at the age of 62, parted with his properties in Grantham. On November 11, 1806 the land records show that lot 13 went to Robert Hamilton, one of the members of the provincial elite and the head of the land office. On the same date, Pierpoint traded lot 12 to Garret Schram, the son of Frederick Schram, a former Ranger. In return, the aging African received 100 acres made up of part of lots 7 and 8 on the second concession in the neighbouring Township of Louth. Sometime after, however, Pierpoint lost this land. The land

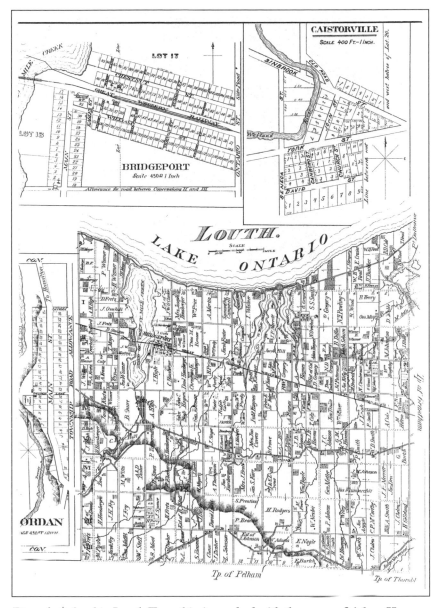

Pierpoint's land in Louth Township is marked with the name of Adam Haynes. Fourteen Mile Creek, which runs through the property, is mislabelled 18 Mile Creek on this map.

Robert Hamilton, one of the most powerful men in the Niagara area, received land beside Pierpoint's. He eventually bought one of Pierpoint's lots in 1806.

records do not show how or when. A registration date of July 30, 1834 for the sale of the land by a John Thompson to Adam Haynes on July 5, 1826 is the next entry on the land registry ledger.[18]

What happened in the twenty years between 1806 and 1826 is not indicated. Did Pierpoint get caught in a land swindle or did he give it away to pay debts? Captain Dick's whereabouts are unknown between 1806 and 1812. He may have lived in the town of Niagara which had about 200 black residents, or he may have housed with friends in Louth or in Grantham Township. The black residents there would have carried on traditions from the African communities in New England and New York, and Pierpoint, as a well-known local resident, would have been an important member of this vibrant community.

In 1812, the United States was threatening the freedom of African Canadians as once more the winds of war were stirring. Richard Pierpoint demonstrated his ongoing concern for this community when he thought of raising a militia compan of African men in the Niagara region. And then, at the age of 68, on September 1, 1812, he prepared for war again as he joined the militia.

6 Partners in Obscurity

In a former industrial district of downtown Toronto, at the corner of Wellington and Portland streets, is a small park built on what was once the old garrison burial yard for nearby Fort York. In the park stands a monument in the shape of a truncated obelisk. Erected on July 1, 1902, plaques on each of the four faces identify the infantry, cavalry and various other specialist regiments which served in the War of 1812.

On the south-west face are listed the regiments which served during the war on the "western frontier," that part of Upper Canada west of Kingston. Crowded into the bottom corner at the very end of the list, so cramped it appears as if added in afterthought, are listed the "Coloured Corps & Indians." The Africans and Natives, allies in war, remain as partners in obscurity.

Yet, it is no real exaggeration to state that without these units, Canada as a nation, at least a nation in its current form, would not exist. War came to the Niagara frontier in the autumn of 1812, following the disastrous, for the Americans, surrender of Fort Detroit in August to General Sir Isaac Brock's British army and Tecumseh's forces from the Shawnee coalition . The Americans would seek to redress this defeat along the Niagara River.

Either in the lead up to the war, or shortly after its declaration on June 18, Richard Pierpoint is credited with sending a petition to Brock requesting permission to raise an all African military unit, "...that all may stand and fight together." [1] Some of the troops may have fought in the upcoming war out of feelings of patriotism, loyalty to the crown, or regimental pride (this and fear of the commanding officer tended to be the key motivations for long-serving professional soldiers), but for the Africans the matter was more fundamental.

All soldiers, of course, shared the risk of death or injury, but the Africans faced a unique threat. Many were ex-slaves or the sons of

This memorial commemorating War of 1812 veterans was erected in 1902. The plaque on this side of the memorial mentions the Coloured Corps. Black veterans held memorial services here into the 1970s.

slaves and, under American law, were viewed as runaways. Even for free men, who never had been slaves, under American law capture did not mean being held as a prisoner of war with eventual repatriation at the end of the conflict. Noncombatants were equally vulnerable. Whatever their status in the British colony, their brown skin ensured they would be treated as property and sold (or resold) into slavery, should they fall into American hands. Freedom for the African residents in the colony was not an abstract concept; the war put their very personal liberty at stake.

The motivation to take up arms against the American invaders, then, is easy to understand. Less clear is Pierpoint's desire to form an all-black company. The British did not segregate their troops, and Africans, both free and slave, served in many various regiments in many various roles. The opportunity to take up arms was not restricted and, as will be recalled, Pierpoint was one of the nineteen free Africans who had sought to form an all-black community in 1794. The reasoning in 1812 was likely the same: to provide mutual protection; to show their loyalty; and to win respect for the African community, further evidence that Pierpoint was willing to take a leadership role in what he saw as a distinct community within the colony.

Pierpoint also may have thought that Africans would be able to advance to higher command more easily within such a unit. During the Revolution it was practically unknown for Africans to hold the rank of a non-commissioned officer (NCO) in the regular or colonial forces, much less hold a commission. Among the Six Nations, however, it was not at all unusual for Africans, or persons of any ethnicity, to attain positions of high responsibility in either civilian or military capacity. Pierpoint also may have been inspired by this example in his efforts to improve the position of Africans in the colony.

If this had been his hope, Pierpoint was to be disappointed. The response to the petition, if there ever was one, has not survived. However, by July, steps were being undertaken to raise such a corps as Pierpoint had suggested. Certainly, General Brock was desperate for more troops and would not lightly turn down any volunteers who appeared at all militarily useful.

One of the few details we know with certainty about the Corps, was that a white man, Captain Robert Runchey, detached from the 2nd Flank Company of the 1st Lincoln militia, was made commander of the unit, which was formally titled "Captain Runchey's Company of Coloured Men." Sergeant George Runchey of the 1st Lincoln was made Lieutenant. No blacks would serve as officers in the unit, although they did fill the positions of NCOs, the sergeants and corporals. In 1812, these included Sergeants Edward Gough and James Watters, along with Corporals Humphrey Waters and Francis Wilson.[2] Pierpoint himself, although now well into his 60s, served as a private in the unit throughout the war. Here age may have been a factor in not being given the additional responsibilities required of an NCO.

Runchey's role with the Corps, in fact, is unclear. It is possible that Runchey was to fill mainly an organizational and training role. He may never have commanded the unit in the field since the only surviv-

The Coloured Corps is remembered on this Ontario government plaque on Queenston Heights. The plaque was originally meant to commemorate the Corps's first commander, Robert Runchey, until it was discovered that his "hero" status was question-nable.

ing records show other officers in charge during combat.[3] Runchey as an officer was not well respected by Colonel Ralph Clench, who at one time commanded the Lincoln militia. He described Runchey as "a Black sheep in our Regiment, and with who the Officers I believe would gladly part."[4] Had Runchey been given the Coloured Corps simply to get him out of the way, or because no one else wanted command of the unit? Had the "black sheep" been given command of black men as a perverse kind of joke? In any case, this scenario suggests the authorities did not have much interest in the corps.

Pierpoint's own service is recorded as starting on September 1, 1812. Seemingly, the idea of the corps was popular among Africans, since, in October, Sergeant William Thompson and thirteen other Africans transferred to the unit from the 3rd York Militia, increasing the strength of the unit to about 35 men. Fighting strength throughout the war averaged 27 to 30 men, in addition to officers. The unit, mostly made up by free black residents of the Niagara area, remained closely associated with the Lincoln militia, which itself was largely officered by veterans or descendants of the Butler's Rangers. Henry Pawling (son of Captain Benjamin Pawling of Butler's Rangers), who

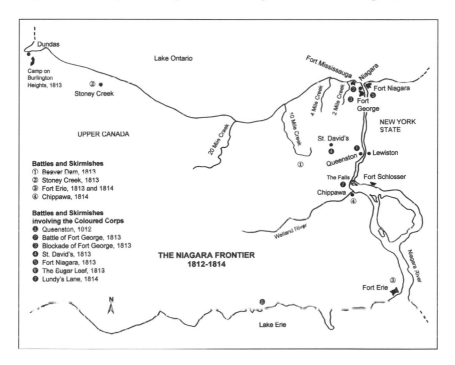

served as a lieutenant in the 1st Lincoln, was chief witness to Pierpoint's will.[5] Pierpoint's Ranger connections remained strong.

Militia units at the time were divided into two categories, the Sedentary Militia, which essentially only existed on paper to supply recruits to the active units, known as the Incorporated Militia. These units, at least, had fairly standardized arms and uniforms, and were given some training. The Coloured Corps was considered to be of the same status as the Incorporated Militia, thus its members were eligible to receive six months pay on discharge. This also meant the unit was expected to take part in all the operations expected of the regular forces.

The military forces of Upper Canada were largely based on the Militia Act of 1808, although Generals Isaac Brock and Roger Hale Sheaffe would later alter some provisions to meet the exigencies of the war, in particular the extension of the terms of service beyond the established six months. The act made all able-bodied males, ages 16 to 60, liable for military service but, except in emergencies, men aged 50 and over would not be called up. Individual companies were to number no less than 20 and no more than 50 men. In peacetime, militia companies would only be gathered together for training once a year, on June 4, the King's birthday. However, the main purpose was to take a census of the fighting strength of a district. As well, militia companies had to be called up for at least two days, but no more than four, during the year for "inspection and exercise." Unlike called-up militia, however, the Coloured Corps was an all-volunteer company.

Pierpoint as a private would have earned a meagre 6 pence a day, after the costs of rations were deducted. A common labourer could expect to earn a daily wage of between 3 to 5 shillings (36 to 60 pence). If a trooper was invalided due to wounds, he would gain an annual pension of £9 (180 shillings). If he was killed, his widow would be eligible for a pension of £5 a year. While officers earned considerably more, military service for the average trooper represented a significant financial sacrifice.

There is little information on how the Corps was outfitted and equipped. Standard line regiments in the regular British army wore red, but rifle units wore green. Specialist units, such as engineers and artillery gunners, wore blue jackets. Militia uniforms were less standardized, depending on uncertain finances, but generally followed regular army patterns. The Coloured Corps, if any standardized uniforms had been provided, may have received red jackets if it was raised as a line company. However, at the Battle of Fort Erie on May 27, 1813, at least one black soldier was killed, who, according to an American officer, was assumed to be a member of the Glengarry militia.[6] This unit, organized as light infantry, wore green jackets (in the regular British army, light infantry wore red jackets, with green reserved for rifle units). Each line regiment had a company of light infantry, seen as a kind of elite made up from the most agile men, and used for skirmishing and other special duties. However, it is possible the American witness was mistaken and the dead soldier may have been from the Coloured Company, which was also present at the battle. The American may have been unaware of the existence of such a relatively small, independent unit. If so, the green jacket may indicate the Corps was established as light infantry, that is, a unit expected to undertake special duties.

As shall be seen, from the scarce documentary evidence, the Corps would seem to have served primarily as skirmishers. It is possible that just as each line regiment had its light company, the Coloured Corps may have fulfilled such a role for the Lincoln militia. One veteran, recalling the war in 1875, thought the name of his colonel was "Clause," likely referring to Lieutenant-Colonel William Claus, commander of the Lincoln militia.[7] Whether or not there was a formal link between the Lincolns and the Corps, it appears that in the minds of some of the men such a connection existed.

Pierpoint's Ranger experience of fighting in the bush would have been of value in this kind of combat, especially for the younger men, so it is useful to examine light infantry fighting in more detail. In combat, the typical light infantry formation, called skirmish order, was a fairly dispersed line based on pairs of soldiers. As one soldier fired, the other loaded. On the attack, the pairs of skirmishers leapfrogged ahead, with the advance of one solider covered by the fire of the other. If enemy pressure became too strong, the skirmishers could retreat in a similar fashion. The goal of the skirmish line was to break up the order of the main enemy line with a continuous harassing fire. Key targets to shoot were officers. Unlike the volley fire of the line troops, where aiming was rudimentary or general, light infantry were expected to aim at specific targets. Also, unlike line infantry, which stood shoulder-to-shoulder, skirmishers were trained to crouch down and make use of cover as much was possible. There was less reliance on the direct commands of officers and more individual initiative was required. The tactics of the Six Nations fighters, considered some of the finest light infantry anywhere, were even more flexible.

Such tactics could prove galling and frustrating for an enemy. As line infantry were expected to stand unmoving in solid ranks, it was rare when they could use cover to avoid enemy fire. On the offence, the power of line infantry was in mass, either by volley fire or by charging. But light infantry, dispersed behind cover, made poor targets; it was wasteful and tiring to make a charge against such troops who could easily withdraw. Line infantry were effectively defenceless against a well-organized light infantry force, unless they were screened by their own skirmish line. A primary goal of light infantry was to eliminate the opposing enemy skirmishers.

By May 1813, the unit had been redesignated as the Provincial Corps of Artificers, military construction troops, but there was little apparent change of duty, and most official returns still referred to the unit as the "Coloured Corps." The regular army artificers uniform was blue, but it would be very unlikely that the Corps received new uniforms merely at the change of designation, particularly when the colonial government was having difficulties giving the troops their basic pay, miserable as that was.

Ideally, militia were to be armed according to the same standards as regular troops, but this standard was not usually achieved. The Corps' principal weapon would have been the Brown Bess smooth-bore musket, which had not changed greatly from the models Pierpoint would have seen during the American Revolution. It is also possible, since priority for arms was given to the regular line troops, that individual militiamen used their own personal firearms, such as hunting rifles, if they possessed them, to make up for any shortages. Such a mix of weapons would have been problematic for volley fire, but would have been less of a problem in a unit of skirmishers.

During the summer of 1812, the Coloured Corps served on the frontier at Fort George. Built between 1796 and 1798, comprising an earthen rampart and wood palisade, Fort George had been located across the Niagara River from the former Butler's Ranger bastion, Fort Niagara, which now lay on the American side of the river (Britain had only given up Fort Niagara to the Americans in 1796). Fort George guarded the town of Niagara, built on the site of Butler's Barracks and, for a short time, capital of Upper Canada.

About ten kilometres upstream from the fort, in the early morning of October 13, an American invasion force under General Stephen van Rensselaer crossed the river and attacked the village of Queenston, which lay just at the foot of the ridge which formed the Niagara gorge. Van Rensselaer commanded about 3000 men in total, but limited transport meant only a fraction of his force could cross the river at one time. The advance guard consisted of about 200 men each from the 13th Regiment (regulars) and from the 19th New York Militia Regiment.

The British garrison, with two companies of regulars from the 49th

Fort George sits quietly across the Niagara River from the American Fort Niagara in this 1800 illustration. The two forts were engaged in battle for the last time twelve years later with the outbreak of the War of 1812.

Regiment and two companies of the York Militia put up a stout resistance. A British 24 pounder cannon, emplaced in a redan on the heights above the village, proved especially troublesome for the Americans. As daylight grew, General Sir Isaac Brock arrived from Fort George in time to repel a new wave of invaders, but only at the cost of weakening the forces at the redan, which, flanked on its east side by the river and ravine, was not considered under immediate threat of attack by the Americans.

The bulk of the garrison of Fort George had been left behind in case this American move was just a feint to cover the main invasion elsewhere. Meanwhile, an enterprising American officer led a small force to scale the steep walls of the ravine and outflank the redan. The surprised gunners were quickly overwhelmed, and the British were faced with disaster as the Americans began to turn their own gun against them.

Brock quickly gathered the light infantry company of the 49th and stormed back up the hill, but men were soon falling to American marksmen; when Brock himself fell fatally wounded, the British retreated back down the slope. But Colonel John Macdonnell of the York militia renewed the charge until he too was shot off his horse

This memorial in the village of Queenston is situated
near the spot where Sir Isaac Brock was shot and
killed during the Battle of Queenston Heights. Close
by is another memorial for Brock's horse, Alfred,
who also died in the battle. Brock's Monument sits
atop the Heights in the background.

with a mortal wound. As news of Brock's death spread, this last
repulse broke the back of the British effort.

The Americans, assuming themselves to have won a victory, set up
fortifying the heights at Queenston, while the labourious work of
ferrying over more troops continued. General Sheaffe, meanwhile, had
ridden to the battlefield and, judging this attack to be no mere feint,
immediately ordered the whole garrison of Fort George to move on
Queenston as quickly as possible.

The first force to arrive were some 160 men from the Six Nations Grand River Reserve under Captains John Norton and John Brant. The latter was the son of Joseph Brant, while Norton was of mixed Cherokee-Scottish background. He had been adopted into the Six Nations and became one of the League's top military leaders. The Six Nations warriors infiltrated though the woods around the heights and began sniping at the Americans clustered about the redan.

The war calls of the Natives alone, announcing the arrival of "Indians," caused a near panic in the American camp. The New York militia units still on the American side, who from the beginning were unenthusiastic about the war, now outrightly refused to cross the river. They argued that under state law they were not obligated to leave their home territory. As British resistance began to strengthen, artillery fire from batteries along the Niagara effectively interdicted any American attempts to ferry troops across. While Van Rensselaer returned to the American side to plead in vain with the militia leaders, Major-General William Wadsworth took command of the battlefield. He now had about 1,000 men in and around Queenston, but his command was, in fact, cut off. The tide of the battle had turned.

It is uncertain exactly when the Coloured Corps arrived on the battlefield. The 30 or so Africans with the light company of the 41st Regiment (altogether about 100 men), sent from Fort George by Sheaffe, were the first reinforcements to reach Norton. At about the same time, some 80 Cayuga warriors arrived upstream from Fort Erie. This inclusion with various other light infantry forces strongly suggests that the Coloured Corps was trained and equipped for skirmishing. The unit was under the field command of Lieutenant James Cooper, an officer with the 2nd Lincoln Militia, apparently a temporary and perhaps emergency appointment. Cooper was later commended for his energetic performance during the battle.[8]

Units from Fort George arrived throughout the afternoon, as the Americans remained virtually paralyzed under the sniping fire of the Natives and Coloured Corps. Units from Forts George and Erie arrived throughout the early part of the afternoon, as the Americans remained virtually paralyzed under the sniping fire of the British light infantry and of with the Africans and Natives; although the Americans did attempt one limited counterattack which inflicted some casualties on the Grand River men. Around three in the afternoon, Sheaffe had enough men to form his line of battle. On the far left were the light company of the 41st Regiments and remnants of the 49th. Just on their right were Norton's men, the Coloured Corps and the 1st and 4th Lincoln Regiments (a placement which appropriately mirrored the earlier alliance between the Six Nations and Butler's Rangers).[9] The centre and right wing were formed out of the remainder of the 41st Regiment and the militia.

The rest of the battle was almost anticlimactic. A concerted advance was made on the American line from the west and southwest, and resistance crumbled. With a gorge behind them there was no retreat, although a few men reportedly threw themselves over the cliff in their panic. Upwards of 900 Americans surrendered. American losses in killed and wounded are not known with accuracy. The British lost 20 killed, 77 wounded and 21 men lost as prisoners. Militia losses are not known, but Norton's force lost five killed, including two Cayuga chiefs, a substantial percentage of the overall total killed.[10]

The Battle of Queenston Heights was decisive in stopping the initial American invasion. Had they succeeded in clearing the Niagara Peninsula, it is uncertain where the British would or could have stopped them. The main British defences were around Montreal and Quebec, then seen as the heart of the Canadian colonies. And, it is questionable if Britain's military leaders, still heavily committed in the fight against Napoleon in Europe, would have diverted substantial resources to hold, much less retake, what was still seen as a somewhat remote western frontier (just as the upper Mississippi west of Detroit had been abandoned after 1783). After Queenston, both London and Washington now realized they were in for a long war.

Next spring, the Americans were back, and this time they could not be stopped. On May 27, a force led by Major-General Henry Dearborn, landed near Two-Mile Creek on the Lake Ontario shore. Already both the town and fort of York, now Toronto, had been taken and burnt in April, and General Sheaffe, with the bulk of the garrison, retreated all the way to Kingston. The British forces on hand, under General John Vincent, were based on the 8th Regiment (310 men), and about 250 militia, including the "Black Corps," as it was called in the report of Captain George Fowler, listed at a strength of 27 men. Fowler, of the 41st Regiment, does not indicate whether or not this figure includes officers or is for rank and file only. The Coloured Corps may have been attached to the 41st at this time, since Gary French in *Men of Colour* indicates Fowler was in command of the unit.[11] American naval gun fire proved decisive, and the small British force was forced back from the beach after taking heavy losses, although again there is no accounting of losses among the militia. Fort George was abandoned and captured by the Americans, although already it was partly in ruins from their bombardment. Fifty-two regulars were killed, 44 wounded and 262 captured, while the Americans lost 39 killed and 111 wounded.[12]

Records for militia losses are fragmentary. Most are based on claims for pensions after the war and, in these cases, only veterans incapacitated by their wounds were eligible. Therefore, lightly wounded soldiers or veterans who did not make a claim for whatever reason, would not be listed. While the anonymous dead African in the green jacket may or may not have served in the Coloured company, there are a few documented casualties which definitely place the unit at the Battle of Fort George. James Walker is listed as having been wounded on May 27, and Anthony Hutts (also given as Hults or Hull) was taken prisoner at the battle. The Americans claimed he later died in captivity, but it is possible Hutts was sold off into slavery and disappeared from official notice either by design or by accident. Americans usually did not treat blacks as prisoners of war, but saw them as any other battlefield loot.

Even more curious is the case of Abraham Sloane and William Spencer, both listed as having deserted to the enemy on May 27. Desertion was common enough in any army of the time and, after the debacle of Fort George, Vincent was faced with serious demoralization among the survivors of his retreating army. But where would black soldiers retreat to? Desertion to the Americans would only lead to enslavement and appears highly improbable. Like Hutts, they could have been captured, wounded or not, and have possibly been sent back to the United States as slaves. Another possibility is that both men were killed and, since the British abandoned the battlefield, their bodies would have been left to the Americans to bury, and were not found again. They would thus be numbered among the many dozens of missing men, which a later historian possibly interpreted as a case of desertion.[13]

The two men could also have fled into the countryside, but two wandering black men would have attracted suspicion at the least in the predominantly white communities of Upper Canada. It should be recalled that slavery was still legal in the colony, and cases of runaway

Fort George was constructed after the British gave up Fort Niagara in 1796. When General Brock took command in 1802, the fort included six bastions, four blockhouses among its many buildings. The stone magazine is the only remaining building from the original fort.

slaves were not unknown. Saving family members could be one possible reason for at least a temporary absence from the ranks. With Vincent's defeat, the large African community of the Niagara Peninsula was now vulnerable to the American invaders. Some men may have attempted to return home in a desperate attempt to save family and friends from American capture.

Combat was not the only hardship faced by the men. Poor rations, exposure to harsh weather and hard labour, all contributed to disease. In another of the few official mentions of the Corps, for example, a Private John Jackson is listed as having died of disease on February 13, 1813, in the winter before the Battle of Fort George.[14]

While many militia battalions were disbanded during the retreat northwest along the shore of Lake Ontario, the proof of the value of the Coloured Corps was that it was kept in service at the encampment on Burlington Heights. It was now under the immediate command of Lieutenant James Robertson, an officer from the Provincial Artificers (army engineers), who had officially taken command of the unit on March 3, 1813. The Corps is rarely mentioned in any narrative sources, but its general movements can be traced through the surviving returns of men fit for duty. After calling in the garrisons of Fort Erie and of Chippawa, General John Vincent had 1,600 men left. On June 3, the Coloured Corps mustered a strength of one captain, three sergeants, and 29 rank and file, with one sick.[15]

The Americans pursued with 3,500 men, but in a surprise British night attack at Stoney Creek where the Native forces again played a key role, the Americans were routed. Even though British losses were higher, 23 killed and 136 wounded to 17 American dead and 38 wounded, the U.S. forces were thoroughly disorganized. Among the 113 prisoners the British captured were two American generals.[16] The American army beat a hasty retreat all the way back to Fort George.

The preceding two weeks had seen an amazing turn in the fortunes of the British. The Americans, who had abandoned the rest of their positions along the Canadian side of the Niagara River, were blockaded in Fort George by a numerically inferior enemy force. Largely in ruins and only partly rebuilt, the fort provided miserable shelter in the hot, humid weather of a southern Ontario summer. Shortly, disease began to further thin the American ranks. Still, with their also depleted numbers, the British could only maintain a loose cordon around the American lines.

The result was sporadic skirmishing in the no man's land between the two hostile encampments, fighting in which the Coloured Corps was again active. On June 10, units of the Lincoln militia possibly accompanied by members of the Coloured company moved to reoccupy Queenston. A patrol of Merritt's Niagara Light Dragoons, a militia cavalry unit, lost four men captured in a skirmish with American forces near the Ten Mile Creek. The Lincoln militia lost six men captured on June 10, while the Coloured listed one casualty.[17] A return for June 13, gives the Corps a strength of two sergeants and 27 rank and file.[18]

By June 15, the Americans had organized a guerrilla force under a Buffalo surgeon, Dr. Cyrenius Chapin. Major Chapin's mounted rifles' purpose was to raid British lines. The British organized a mobile counterforce of their own, based on Merritt's dragoons and other militia volunteers, possibly including men from the Lincoln militia and Coloured Corps. On June 16, Chapin's force raided deep into British territory, and surprised some enemy forces 15 kilometres west of Fort Erie at what was called the Sugar Loaf (near present day Port Colborne). The Lincoln militia lost six men captured there, while five men from various other units were recorded as also having been captured at the Sugar Loaf. As well, the Coloured Corps lists three casualties on June 16, but it is not known whether in this battle or a related action.[19] The three are again listed as having deserted, but with British fortunes on an upswing this would be even more unlikely than before Fort George, so it is possible these men were captured by Chapin's raiders.

The Americans next determined to make a major sortie to regain the initiative and, on June 23, a strong force of about 600 men set out to surprise the British garrison near the Ten Mile Creek. But the Americans were themselves surprised at Beaver Dams by an ambush of a mixed force of Six Nations from the Grand River and from Montreal. American morale was now thoroughly broken and no major offensive actions were taken for the remainder of the campaigning season, although intermittent skirmishing continued. The Coloured Corps served throughout the summer and fall at the blockade of Fort George. One surviving return from August 22, 1813, gives a total of one officer and 26 rank and file fit for duty,[20] while another, for September 15, lists a strength of one officer, 22 rank and file and 4 sick.[21]

On December 10, the American forces abandoned Fort George and fell back across the river, but not before burning Niagara and devastating the surrounding farm land. The British quickly followed up and surprised the Americans, so that their work of destruction was halted prematurely and the barracks at Fort George were captured intact. A quick push across the river led to the easy capture of the American Fort Niagara, as well as the elimination of the batteries at Lewiston and Schlosser. By the end of December, Buffalo itself had fallen.

The Coloured Corps was given the task of helping to rebuild Fort George, but their primary task was the construction of an entirely new redoubt to cover the mouth of the Niagara River, called Fort Mississauga. It was not only strenuous but hazardous work, both due to the weather and nearby enemy garrisons. As artificers, the corps was also responsible for digging battlefield earthworks and entrenchments. This type of work was often done under enemy fire and artificers earned four or five times the typical pay of a regular soldier. It is unclear if the Corps ever received this "danger" pay. One private, Peter Lee, was recorded as having been injured in an accident on March 10, 1814, at Fort Niagara.[22] This would indicate that the Coloured Corps was also active here, adding and rebuilding the

The only shots heard around Fort Mississauga these days are from the golf course which border it on three sides. The earthwork embankments constructed with the help of Captain Dick surround the remaining building.

partially destroyed American fortifications. As the main defences at the fort had been rebuilt after 1796 to face the British frontier across the river, new landward defences had to be constructed.

To give some idea of the importance and type of work done by the artificers, in a report from July 3, Fort Mississauga was described as almost complete, with the outer works done and a brick tower started. Fort George, however, due to lack of manpower, was still in a state of disrepair and was considered indefensible. Fort Niagara was given new defences and palisading on the landward side, to face any potential American attack. However, Fort Mississauga was left as the main defence at the mouth of the Niagara. General Sir Gordon Drummond felt it could stand up to a land assault, but could not survive a concerted artillery bombardment.[23]

Meanwhile, morale of the garrison in Fort Niagara plummeted along with the temperature in the winter of 1813-14. Monotonous duty and the fact that back pay was also owed for six months did not help. Desertion became rife. Of the four companies on garrison at Fort Niagara, with a combined strength of 324 men, a total of 45 men were listed as absent on December 15, 1813.[24] However, there are no recorded losses from the Coloured Company that winter.

Following the failed British spring offensive against Oswego, the American army, under General Jacob Brown, counterattacked that summer and cleared the Niagara River of British garrisons, starting from Buffalo and Fort Erie. Following the defeat of General Phineas Riall at Chippawa, the main British army abandoned the river and fell back to Twenty Mile Creek. The Coloured Corps, (its strength on June 22, 1814 was listed as one officer, 2 sergeants, 20 rank and file and four sick),[25] was left behind as part of the garrison at Fort Mississauga. In an effort to draw Riall's forces into another battle, the Americans threatened forts George and Mississauga. The former was really indefensible, had the Americans pressed their attack. The only really defendable strongpoint left on the Niagara River for the British was Fort Mississauga. However, fearing for his lines of communications and with no sign of the U.S. squadron on Lake Ontario, Brown began to fall back to Queenston. Riall pursued and the two forces collided in the confused and bloody battle of Lundy's Lane. The last known return for the Coloured Corps dates from July 8, 1814, and gives the unit a strength of one officer, two sergeants, a drummer, 22 rank and file and four sick. The Coloured Corps came under the command of Major Thomas Evans, of the 8th Regiment, commander of the Fort Mississauga garrison.[26]

The evidence of one veteran, Simon Groat, shows the Coloured Corps fought at Lundy's Lane.[27] The unit was by now a proven and veteran unit. Any field works at the battle would likely have been the responsibility of the Coloured Corps. The unit formed part of Tucker's Brigade which included all the garrisons of the forts along the lakeshore near the mouth of the Niagara. As the British army concentrated northwest of Queenston, Lieutenant Colonel Tucker was ordered to split his forces. Leaving a small garrison behind, one column was sent directly to support Riall, while the other advanced on Lewiston on the American side of the Niagara. Having quickly defeated the American garrison here, the bulk of Tucker's force recrossed the river and joined up with the main army.

The Battle of Lundy's Lane began at 6 p.m. on July 25, 1814, and lasted well after midnight, unusual for the time when most fighting stopped after dark. The British lost 81 dead, 562 wounded and 233 missing, while the Americans suffered 171 dead, 573 wounded and 117 missing. It proved to be the bloodiest battle of the entire conflict, but the result was a draw. However, for the Americans, who needed a clear victory, it proved to be a strategic defeat and their retreat continued, although the British were too exhausted to mount much of a pursuit.[28]

That was the last major action on the Niagara frontier. The Coloured Corps continued in service at Fort Mississauga until the declaration of peace, which came with the signing of the Treaty of Ghent in 1814. Hostilities did not actually end until early 1815, however, and the Corps was not disbanded until March 24, 1815.

The Corps had seen action at most of the major battles on the Niagara frontier. The unit had played an important role at Queenston in 1812. The men had survived defeat and retreat in 1813. They had built and partly garrisoned Fort Mississauga, the bastion that anchored the British frontier defences during the crisis of the summer of 1814. Battle, disease and mischance, as in any other combat unit, had taken its toll.

Pierpoint, now aged 71 in 1815, had survived it all. But the War of 1812 was similar to many other conflicts in that the veterans were soon forgotten. For the Coloured Corps, military service had not won honour and respect. At least, the historical record has almost left the unit in oblivion. Reintegration into civilian life would not be easy. For most veterans, the war was a financial disaster, even if they did not lose their farms, as many did along the frontier, to enemy devastation.

In part, the six month's discharge bonus was designed to help veterans survive until they could find work or bring in a new crop. But the cash-strapped colonial authorities, faced with recovering from what had been a devastating war, were not in a hurry to pay. Pierpoint had fought against the American invaders for three years to preserve his freedom. He now faced an even longer fight against the very government he had defended, to win the recognition of his rights as a soldier and citizen.

7   Home on the Grand

Upper Canada was rapidly evolving after the War of 1812. A major influx of immigrants pushed the population from 75,000 in 1815 to over 200,000 by 1830. With much of the growth occurring in the western part of the province, Kingston was still the largest city, but York's population increased fourfold to 2,800. After the war, Pierpoint lived in the town of Niagara, a town with a very diverse population. The newspaper publisher and political reformer, William Lyon Mackenzie, described this 1824 election crowd in Niagara:

> "There were Christians and Heathens, Menonists and Dunkards, Quakers and Universalists, Presbyterians and Baptists, Roman Catholics and American Methodists; there were Frenchmen and Yankees, Irishmen, and Mulattoes, Scotchmen and Indians, Englishmen, Canadians, Americans and Negroes, Dutchmen and Germans, Welshmen and Swedes, Highlanders and Lowlanders, poetical as well as most prosaical phises, horsemen and footmen, fiddlers and dancers, honourables and reverends, captains and colonels, beaux and belles, waggons and bilburies, coaches and chaises, gigs and carts; in short, Europe, Asia, Africa, and America had there each its representative among the loyal subjects of our good King George, the fourth of the name."[1]

There, the African-Canadian presence was still important to the area. The connections to the military and the old guard in the province were still present, as demonstrated in October of 1824 when General Brock's body was moved from Fort George to Queenston Heights. The three hour prossession, which included all of the province's elite and the Six Nations leaders, was led by African Canadians. A witness of the event recalled that the hearse was a large army wagon drawn by four black horses, driven by a black driver, and four black men walked by the side of the horses.[2]

With American blacks continuing to spill across the border, escaping the brutal American slavery system, the province's African settlements continued to grow. One such site for black homesteaders only was set up by Lieutenant Governor Sir Peregrine Maitland in 1819. Placed strategically between Lake Simcoe and Georgian Bay in Oro Township near present day Barrie, the community would act as a buffer if the Americans ever invaded through the upper Great Lakes. Most of the several hundred African pioneers received land along the second concession road which had been named Wilberforce Street after the famous British abolitionist. Included were War of 1812 veterans, American refugees and even immigrants from the Caribbean. Other settlements, by necessity, were established in the unsurveyed areas of southwestern Ontario. Known as the Queen's Bush, this territory stretched from present day Kitchener-Waterloo west to Lake Huron and north to Georgian Bay. Artemesia Township, midway between Lake Ontario and Georgian Bay, had a large black population as did its neighbouring townships. But probably the largest black community of the time was developing in the adjoining counties of Wellington and Waterloo. By 1847, there were up to 1,500 African settlers spread over 72 square miles in the townships of Peel, Woolwich and Wellesley. This locale, known only as the Queen's Bush settlement, grew considerably during the 1830s.[3]

There were no lists of residents of the Queen's Bush while Pierpoint was living in Garafraxa. However, he would have known at least two settlers that were known to be there in subsequent years. One was Sophia Burthen Pooley. A native of Fishkill, New York on the Hudson River, she had been taken from her parents and sold to Joseph Brant in the Niagara area sometime before the Revolution. Only about seven years old when she became a slave of the Mohawk leader, she worked for the Brant family for a number of years. During this time she was sure to have become acquainted with Pierpoint. She knew his Coloured Corps comrade, John Van Patten, since his father was also one of Brant's servants. Another familiar name that shows up is that of Simon Groat, the same name as a member of the Coloured Corps.

It is likely that Pierpoint knew other blacks in the Queen's Bush as well as residents in Oro and Artemesia townships.[4] It is said that Pierpoint travelled widely. Known and respected by many, he had taken on the role of a 'griot' (an oral historian who keeps and passes on the

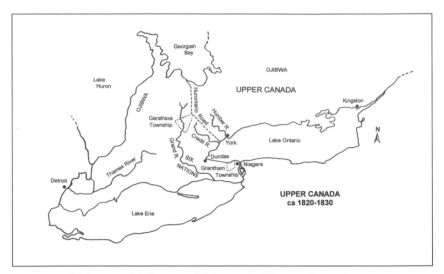

history of his people) for the Africans in Upper Canada.

Many of Upper Canada's new immigrants, however, came directly from the British Isles and knew little about the land that they were coming to, let alone the history of the people who made up the population. The typical European view of American Indians and Africans was that they were inferior to Europeans, with many considering them savages and heathens. Such enthocentric views led to a more marginalized role for both of these groups in the changing society as the new arrivals competed for land and jobs. For Pierpoint, now a man in his seventies, the competition for work would have been especially difficult.

In the spring of 1820, important news from the colonial government reached the War of 1812 veterans in Niagara. For Richard Pierpoint, the news was both bad and good. It was good in that his military service with the Coloured Corps was finally being recognized and rewarded. The down side for Captain Dick was that the reward was a 100 acre "grant of the waste lands of the Crown" in a recently surveyed area along the Grand River.[5]

For a younger man, the chance to own land might have brought hope for a better future but, for the 76 year old native of Bundu, the past weighed more heavily on his mind than the future. Pierpoint's aspiration at the time of hearing the news was to find a way home to Bundu, not to start over on a new piece of land. The hope of returning to his homeland was still there, even though he had been gone for over 60 years.

Joseph Brant's house, in Burlington, Ontario, was on the route between Niagara and York (now Toronto) and would have been well known to Pierpoint. Michael Groat bought 140 acres of the Brant property in 1807. He may be the same Groat or a relative of the Michael Grote who signed the petition of 1794.

By the summer of that year, Captain Dick had a plan to fulfil his wish. He travelled the well-worn road from Niagara, around the tip of Lake Ontario past Joseph Brant's house in Burlington, to the capital, York. He carried with him a carefully drafted petition destined for the King's representative in Upper Canada, Lieutenant Governor Maitland. The handwritten petition is the most important historical document relating to the old African since it outlines Richard Pierpoint's life. It reads:

"The Petition of Richard Pierpoint, now of the Town of Niagara, a Man of Colour, a native of Africa, and an inhabitant of this Province since 1780.

Most humbly showeth,

That your Excellency's Petitioner is a native of Bondou in Africa; that at the age of Sixteen Years he was made a Prisoner and sold as a Slave; that he was conveyed to America about the year 1760, and sold to a British officer; that he served his Majesty during the American Revolutionary War in the Corps called Butler's Rangers; and again during the late American War in a Corps of Colour raised on the Niagara Frontier.

That Your Excellency's Petitioner is now old and without property; that he finds it difficult to obtain a livelihood by his labour; that he is above all things desirous to return to his native Country; that His Majesty's Government be graciously pleased to grant him any relief, he wishes it may be affording him the means to proceed to England and from thence to a Settlement near the Gambia or Senegal Rivers, from whence he could return to Bondou...[6]

On July 21, 1821, Pierpoint visited the Adjutant General's office in Fort York. The Adjutant General of the Militia, Lieutenant Colonel Nathaniel Coffin, added a personal recommendation which confirmed Pierpoint's service and found him to be "faithful and deserving." He also wrote "that the said Richard Pierpoint, better known by the name of Captain Dick was the first colored man who proposed to raise a Corps of Men of Color on the Niagara Frontier, in the last American War."[7] As demonstrated through all of his life in Canada, Captain Dick's military stature in the colony, is validated by this document.

Whether due to a lack of interest, since Africans were not highly regarded by most Europeans at that time, or due to a lack of funds, since the colonial government continually had fiscal problems, the petition was not acted upon. What the government was most interested in at this time, was the opening up of the Queen's Bush area of the province. This territory was, of course, already inhabited by the Ojibwa people who had lived there since the Huron had left in the 1600s. As well, many squatters lived across this extensive wilderness area. Many of these were the African Americans needing to avoid contact with white people for fear of being kidnapping and returned to slavery.

The ongoing threat of U.S. expansion and the pressure of American immigration combined to push the government into initiating more formal and controlled settlement. In 1819, surveyors were contracted to start the process of laying out the concessions and plotting the 200 acre lots in the new townships. The government wanted to settle the new areas with people who would be loyal to the British Crown. Descendants of United Empire Loyalists and those who had fought for the Crown during the War of 1812 were the obvious choice to receive land.

In 1821, Richard Pierpoint met Lieutenant Colonel Nathaniel Coffin in York with his petition to return home to Bundu. The meeting likely took place in the offices in this building in Fort York.

Regular soldiers were entitled to grants and, in 1819, government policy changed to allow militia men to receive land as well. They would receive a militia certificate, confirming their military service, which would be taken to the Surveyor General's office where a lot would be located on a survey map. The office would then issue a Location Ticket to the veteran. This ticket specified the lot and also listed the settlement duties that were required to receive title to the property. With the ticket in hand, the war veteran would have the often arduous task of finding his piece of land. Help was often required to determine the exact location of a lot among the forests that covered the undulating landscape of the southwestern Ontario. There were few roads and the blazed trails left by the surveyors may have disappeared in the years before settlement.

Veterans of the War of 1812 received grants in various parts of the province. Eleven veterans, including six former Coloured Corps members, received 100 acre lots in Oro Township. Many of them never settled in the remote township but leased or sold their land to others. Coloured Corps veteran George Martin, whose father had been a slave of John Butler and a Butler's Ranger, received a grant in

Mono Township.[8] Martin's grant was for the west half of lot 7 in the 2nd concession east of Hurontario Street which had been planned as the main route from York to Owen Sound. He lived in Niagara and had no desire to move to this area, so in 1831 he sold his land to another Niagara resident, David Thorburn.

Captain Dick was one of three Coloured Corps veterans, all with connections to Butler's Rangers, who received grants in the recently surveyed township called "Garrafraxa,"[9] a Native word meaning panther country. John Van Patten, the son of one of Joseph Brant's slaves, received half of lot 4 on the first concession. He had been a corporal with the Coloured Corps. His land ticket was located on April 19, 1822 and, by May 22, 1823, he had fulfilled the required duties of clearing and fencing five acres and constructing a house. This was probably accomplished with the help of other members of the African and Six Nations communities. Shortly after finishing his settlement duties, he sold his land, and returned home. According to his land grant, he lived in the "Indian Land of the County of Haldimand,"[10] and may have been working for the Secords in the Burlington area at the time.

Robert Jupiter had served with the Coloured Corps and was a corporal by the end of the war. He had been a slave of the Daniel Servos family of the Niagara area, but had been so well respected that on his death he was buried in the Servos family burial ground. After the war, he lived in Chippawa, a village west of Niagara Falls, where he had work, a wife and children. As his land grant was in an isolated area of Garafraxa Township, Jupiter had asked the government to find another location for him. The government agent's reply, dated April 9, 1824, read, "Neither Mr. Mercer nor I could find a better lot for Jupiter than the one I have located, it is in a valuable township, though rather remote."[11] The government's letter came too late for Jupiter, however, he had died that same month. His settlement duties went uncompleted and his family never received title to the land.

When Captain Dick's lot was located on July 30, 1822, the clearing of land had already begun and a small African community was forming. Unlike the other Coloured Corps veterans who had decided not to settle on their new properties, Pierpoint did not have family ties or steady work and, not having received a positive reply to his petition, he set out for his new property.

The picturesque Grand River cut through the middle of his lot. Ojibwa traversed the area, moving through their seasonal hunting,

Richard Pierpoint's name appears on the 1821 plan for Garafraxa Township. His neighbour on the west, Harvey Norton, was also from the Niagara area. Three members of the Wintermute family received land north of him. A number of the Wintermute family had been members of Butler's Rangers.

fishing and farming grounds. Bald eagles and great blue herons balanced in the tall elms and walnut trees that competed with the cedars hugging the riverbanks. Numerous springs bubbled through the ground and provided a year long supply of water. Game was plentiful; turtle, deer, beaver and porcupine would soon grace the tables of the new settlers. Still, five acres of trees needed to be cleared, not only to fulfil the settlement duties, but also to provide room for the planting of crops.

Pierpoint would not have been able to accomplish his settlement duties without help. He was 81 years old by 1825, and was not always in the best of health. He needed help in raising crops and taking care of his property. This help came from a younger man known as Deaf Moses. Letters in the James Webster family, one of the founders of Fergus, mention Deaf Moses,[12] and indicate that he helped Pierpoint in his Garafraxa home. His nickname came as a result of hearing loss, caused by being too close to a cannon blast during the War of 1812.

In an old history of West Garafraxa Township, the first settlers were said to have arrived in 1826. We know this is not true since land had been cleared prior to this. These early settlers, whose family name was Dobbin, left the following description of their trek in July 1826 from present day Elora to their land on the 7th concession: "...followed the Indian Trail from home of Roswell Matthews...to father's lot, which was 16 miles, without seeing the face of a white man."[13] From this description it would appear that while the Dobbins may have seen other people on their walk, they weren't white. Such others may have been some of the early African settlers.

One of the first black settlers in the area may have been Robert Scott, a man listed as a member of the Coloured Corps.[14] A Mr. Scott, known as "the Contractor" built the first house in Fergus for Adam Ferguson's Scottish settlers in 1833. While the construction was going on, William Buist, the Scotsman for whom the new house was being erected, stayed in Scott's house. This would suggest that Scott was already resident in the area before the Scots arrived. It would seem that Scott was also the contractor responsible for building the first bridge across the Grand River in Fergus.[15] There is no indication of who this Mr. Scott was or where he came from in any local histories, even though he played an integral part in the establishing of the town. If he was black, it is possible that there would have been little interest in recording his story as part of the area's history.

The Grand River cut through Captain Dick's property which is located halfway up the river from this vantage point on the Black Bridge. The bridge is aligned with the old Garafraxa Road which marked the border of the original land grant to the Six Nations after the American Revolution.

In addition to Pierpoint's old friends from Niagara, it is likely that American refugees would have assisted him in Garafraxa. Needing to find a place to live and settle, many of them moved north into the Queen's Bush area. Their journeys were helped by African-Canadians, and the remote township of Garafraxa would have been a good place to find refuge. There, farm produce, as well as wild game, could be shared with the increasing number of blacks escaping from the United States. The Garafraxa route led to Owen Sound, and many African settlers started farms in the unsurveyed Queen's Bush between Garafraxa and Georgian Bay. The black settlement along the Grand by Fergus would make a natural stopover for a weary traveller. Here they had a chance to rest and receive guidance on the route to follow to go farther north. Letters in the James Webster family indicate that there were a number of black residents in the area. Those without land grants may have helped clear and farm the land for other Niagara area war veterans. Altogether, a total of 1,600 acres belonged to just three of the well-to-do families from that area. Robert, Jacob and Abraham Servos had each been granted 200 acres, as had Nathan, Peter, John and Benjamin Pawling. As well, four war veterans from John Butler's family received 800 acres in the new township. All three of these families were descended from officers in Butler's Rangers, and all had had close connections to the black community in the Niagara area.

There were long days of burning underbrush, sawing trees and hauling logs. It was not unusual for the black women to help with this arduous labour because of their experience as slaves. They had performed hard manual labour on farms and plantations and were more than just capable.

At the end of the day, communal dinners were prepared by the new settlers. After dinner they would gather to sing, play music and to hear Captain Dick tell stories about the history and culture of his homeland. Age is very revered in African culture and elders, such as Pierpoint, would be held in high esteem. One of the people who listened to the stories of Pierpoint while in Garafraxa, was the great-great-grandmother of Howard Sheffield in Collingwood. To this day, the Sheffield family still recounts stories about Pierpoint.[16]

On May 9, 1825, the road, the house which was at least 16 feet by 20 feet, and the five acre clearing, were sworn to have been completed by John Brown and Levi Johnson from Waterloo Township.[17] Captain Dick could now claim ownership to his one hundred acre lot. Exactly where his cabin was located is unknown. However, Lamond Street which passes in front of John Black Public School, just outside of Fergus, probably led to it. This road at one time led to a bridge that crossed the river at the first concession and was the main road between Fergus and Orangeville. In the winter of 1835, A.D. Ferrier and Alex Drysdale, two early European settlers, stayed in a cabin that may have been Pierpoint's. It is described as being east of Fergus and close to the river. Ferrier described the winter conditions in the cabin. He told of how the temperatures dropped to -30 degrees and that everything in the cabin would freeze. The fireplace was kept going all the time and the cabin would fill with smoke since the door needed to be kept closed to keep wolves out. There was a spring close to the cabin which was used to thaw frozen meat. The meat was placed in a box with holes in it and the box would be suspended in the flowing waters. Food was cooked over the fireplace in a big, black pot or the bake kettle.[17]

It is likely that Pierpoint and his compatriots only lived in the Garafraxa settlement during the summer and moved back to the

The Niagara area had a vibrant black community in the 1820s and '30s. This view of Queenston Heights shows Brock's Monument as it looked in 1834 near the end of Pierpoint's life. In 1824, General Brock's body was moved from its original burial place in Fort George to his monument. The procession from the fort to the heights was led by six African-Canadians on black horses.

more settled Niagara region after planting the fall wheat crop in September. The Niagara area with its active African community would have provided more support and amenities for Captain Dick. The settlement in Garafraxa, by contrast, was very isolated and would have been difficult to access. A contemporary description of the route from the settlement to nearest store which was in the village of Dundas highlights this problem:

"...only road to Dundas was the Indian Path to the settlement in Pilkington, then on the Path to Waterloo, then by Bush Road past John Erb's Mill now in Preston, through Beverly Township near where the gravel road runs from Galt."[18]

The spring would see the return of Pierpoint to his land along the Grand River. The livestock would be let loose to wander through the woods, grazing on whatever they could find. Crops, such as rye, oats, peas, barley and corn needed to be planted. The fall wheat crop needed to be taken care of as well. Wheat was an important commodity since it could be distilled into whiskey, one of the few products that could easily be sold for cash. At the end of summer, the wheat for the following spring would be planted and Pierpoint would return to Niagara. The old African settled into this rhythm of following the seasons between Niagara and Garafraxa for his remaining years.

8   The Journey Home

Winter hugged the Niagara area with its cold Arctic winds in January of 1828. The creaking of the frozen pine branches against a lifeless sky must have reminded an elderly man of his own mortality. Henry Pawling was carefully writing out the last will and testament of his old friend, Richard Pawpine. The will indicated that Pawpine had no heirs or relations, all of his worldly possessions were to be left to a farmer named Lemuel Brown.[1] One of Pawpine's possessions was a farm on the east half of lot 6 on the first concession in Garafraxa Township. This, of course, was the property of Richard Pierpoint. The last name on the will was spelled as it would have sounded pronounced with the soft African accent of what seems to be the French pronunciation of Pierpoint.

The author of the will, Henry Pawling, who lived in Louth Township, had probably known the old man all of his life but only as Captain Dick. Pawling was a descendant of a member of Butler's Rangers. The two witnesses of the will, Peter and John Ten Broeck were also part of a family with connections to Butler's Rangers. An 'X' and a thumbprint were left by Pierpoint at the end of the document to indicate his approval of its contents.

As for Brown, the sole beneficiary in the will, we know little about him. Who he was or why he was left all of the Captain's property is not known. He obviously helped the old African somehow in his later years. There were a few Browns listed in the Coloured Corps, so he may have been related to them. Brown had a large family and, at the time that the will was written, lived in Pierpoint's old township of Grantham. The 1828 census shows eleven people in the Brown household, seven males and four females. Perhaps Captain Dick lived with Brown and was one of the four males over sixteen years of age shown in the records. The name Richard Pierpoint does not show up in the Grantham census, even though his will shows that he had property there. Curiously, there is a Frederick W. Pierpoint listed in the Louth Township census of that year.

This is my last Will and Testament
in the name of God Amen
I have no heirs nor relations
I Make Lemuel Brown my heir
and Exeutor I do give to Lemuel
Brown the one half of Lot Number
Six in the first Concession of Garafax-
aw Containing one hundred acres to
him his heirs Administrators and assigns
forever I Like wise give Lemuel Brown
Lot No Thirteen in the eight Concession
of Grantham in the Destrict of Niagara to him his heirs and administrators and
signs forever I like wise Do give Lemuel
Brown his heirs and Assigns all Real
and Personel property to him his heirs
and assigns and administrators forever
to make use of as he thinks proper

The two page will of Captain Dick indicated that he had no living family in 1828. A thumbprint after the name Richard Pawpine is the only physical artifact of the old African who had spent over 75 years in North America.

This I make my last will being
weak but in my perfect Sences
Therefore I put my hand and Seal
this twentieight day of January
in the year eighteen hundred and
twenty eight I set my hand and Seal
Witneses

Richard Pawtine

Henry Pawtney

Witneses

Wellington County had a number of black residents, including William Groat. William Groat was a son of Michael Groat, who had purchased some of Joseph Brant's land in Burlington. A man named Simon Groat lived in Peel Township in the 1840s. The Coloured Corps also had a member named Simon Groat.

Captain Dick spent the remaining years of his life travelling throughout the colony, visiting his many acquaintances and friends. He resided in both the Niagara and Garafraxa areas with his aide, Deaf Moses. In his 94th year, the old African finally went home, for in late 1837 or early 1838 he passed away.

It has been a source of debate as to where Pierpoint died and was buried. Some have thought that he remained in the St. Catharines area and died there. But, there are no reports of his death in the local papers in the Niagara region even though he was a well-known figure. Almost twenty years after his death, an article in the *St. Catharines Journal* of July 31, 1856 contained the following paragraph:

"Captain Dick (colored) who owned one hundred acres, near by, was said to have buried a considerable amount of money; and when, on his death-bed, tried to disclose its whereabouts, but was too far gone, and failed. The property changed, in the course of time into several hands, and if report be true, each one has

This view of Fergus shows the town as it looked at the end of Richard Pierpoint's life. St. Andrew's Church can be seen just above the stump on the right hand side of the illustration.

ploughed, digged, uprooted and ransacked it pretty freely and pretty fully."

On September 27, 1838, Lemuel Brown was in the Niagara court-house with the will of Richard Pawpine. Around this time Deaf Moses was in Fergus, hired by James Webster. Also at this time, Webster had a dispute with the members of the only church in Fergus, St. Andrew's Presbyterian. Webster had requested that someone who wasn't named be buried in the churchyard. The church members would only allow this person to be buried in an unmarked grave in the pauper's field.[3] There must have been compelling reasons for the church members to turn down Webster, one of the founders of the town. Webster wouldn't agree to a burial in a pauper's grave. It may well have been Webster's old African acquaintance who was the subject of the dispute.

When the will was probated, Brown had moved from Grantham and was living in Halton County. The will left two land holdings to Brown. The one hundred acre lot in Garafraxa was sold in the spring of 1839 by Lemuel Brown and his wife to Alex Drysdale, the owner of the neigbouring farm. The will also left lot 23 on the eighth concession of Grantham Township to Lemuel. The land records did not substantiate

Pierpoint's ownership of this lot; land ownership in the Niagara region was not always registered or well documented in the early years of the colony. Brown's claim was officially turned down in 1844 and that was the last official mention of Richard Pierpoint: slave, soldier, settler.

For almost 150 years there was little interest in writing about this remarkable man. The legacy of African settlers in Canada were almost never included in books about the country's settlement and, when they were mentioned, it was usually in passing and quite often derogatorily. With waves of immigrants from various backgrounds researching their place in this continent's history, things have started to change. The heroic deeds of Africans in North America are coming to the forefront. There is an African saying, "Only when lions have historians will hunters cease being heroes." The lions now have their historians.

Notes

INTRODUCTION

1 These small doorways were called doors of return because those who went through them, generally never returned. For more information see: Steven Barboza, *Door of No Return*. New York: Cobblehill Books, 1994.

1 THE WELLSPRING

1 Constance Jones, *Africa*. (New York: Facts on File, 1993) 78 79, 82; and Louise Minks, *Traditional Africa*. (San Diego: Lucent Books, 1996) pp 60-63. Jones gives an estimate of 100,000 slaves per year for the trans-Atlantic slave trade alone between 1700 and 1800. Minks gives an average of 15 million slaves from about 1500 to 1880, but notes that some historians double or treble that figure. She also provides some national breakdown of figures with Spain transporting 7000 slaves per year and Portugal 10,000 per year to their New World colonies. Britain, in the late 1700s, transported 40,000 slaves per year. But all of these figures, due to incomplete or inaccurate accounting, must be taken as estimates, and those figures that are documented only include those Africans that reached the European trading networks. The number of people that died before reaching the European posts is unknown.

2 The original petition is in the National Archives of Canada. A copy is found in: Headly Tulloch, *Black Canadians*. (Toronto: New Canada Publications, 1975) 98.

3 Douglas Grant, *The Fortunate Slave*. (London: Oxford University Press, 1968). The story of Ayuba Sulayman Diallo was first published in Francis Moore's *Travels into the Inland Parts of Africa* in 1738. The chapter entitled 'The History of Job ben Solomon' was the impetus for Grant's research into Sulayman's life.

4 Michael A. Gomez, *Pragmatism in the Age of Jihad, The Precolonial State of Bundu*. (Cambridge: Cambridge University Press, 1992) 56 58. Gomez has written perhaps the only comprehensive history of Bundu in English.

5 Grant, 81.

6 Gomez, 70; Grant, 46-47.

7 Gomez, 27; Grant, 64.

8 Grant, 68.

9 C. Becker, "Kayor and Baol: Bengalese Kingdoms and the Slave Trade in the 18th Century," *Forced Migration,* (Hutchinson University Library for Africa, 1982) 107-111. This relatively small region alone delivered an average of 500 slaves per year to the French trade system.

2 THE TIME OF TERROR

1 Douglas Grant, *The Fortunate Slave*, 53.
2 The term factory came from the title of the trading company officer, the factor, who administered the post.
3 Grant, 70-71.
4 Ibid, 77.
5 Eveline Christiana Martin, *The British West African Settlements, 1750-1821; A Study in Local Administration,* (London: Longman Grant & Co., 1927) 8-10.
6 Ibid, 38-41 and 70-71. This highlights the problem of the illegal or unofficial trade in slaves, which would tend to indicate that any official figures on the number of people taken as slaves would be lower than the actual number.
7 Ann Rinaldi, *Hang a Thousand Trees with Ribbons: The Story of Phillis Wheatley* (San Diego/New York/London: Harcourt Brace & Co., 1996) unnumbered frontispiece.
8 Grant, 73.
9 Grant, 74; Martin, 27.
10 William D, Pierson, *Black Yankees.* (Amherst: The University of Massachusetts Press, 1988) 9.
11 Michael A. Gomez, *Pragmatism in the Age of Jihad, The Precolonial State of Bundu,* 22-23; Grant, 81.

3 A PIECE OF PROPERTY

1 Douglas Grant, *The Fortunate Slave*, 81.
2 Ibid.
3 Ann Rinaldi, *Hang a Thousand Trees with Ribbons: The Story of Phillis Wheatley,* unnumbered frontispiece.
4 William D, Pierson, *Black Yankees*, 39.
5 Ibid, 75.
6 Ibid, 15-18.
7 Sherrill D. Wilson, *New York City's African Slaveowners.* (New York: Garland Publishing Inc., 1994) 47-48.
8 Pierson, 49-50.
9 Ibid, 74.
10 Ibid,103.
11 Wilson, 66-67.
12 Jack D. Forbes, Black Africans and Native Americans: Color, Race, and Caste in the Evolution of Red-Black Peoples. (New York and Oxford: Basil Blackwell, 1988) 192-193.
13 *Molly Brant: Woman of Two Worlds,* pamphlet produced by the State of New York Office of Parks, Recreation and Historic Preservation (Not dated).
14 The Johnson Papers, Vol. V, 759. Robarts Reference Library, University of Toronto.

4 THE RHYTHM OF WAR

1 Allan Woolley, *Butler's Rangers, Crown Forces in America 1775-1783.* (http://iaw.on.ca/awoolley/brang/brang.html, 1998).

2 Ernest Cruikshank, *Butler's Rangers.* (Niagara Falls: Lundy's Lane Historical Society, 1893, reprinted 1988) 37.

3 Ibid, 37.

4 Ibid, 50.

5 Ibid, 87.

6 Joseph R. Fischer, *A Well Executed Failure.* Columbia: University of South Carolina Press, 1997) 108-111.

7 Pontiac, an Ottawa chief, lead a coalition of western nations against the British in 1763. This uprising began in reaction to the British assumption of ownership of Native lands whose independence had been recognized by the French. Pontiac's coalition had managed to capture eight of the twelve posts before a peace settlement was reached in 1766. William Johnson played a key role in stopping this frontier ws from moving east by maintaining the neutrality of the Six Nations.

8 _____, Richard Pierpoint biographical summary, St. Catharines Historical Museum, May 29, 1985.

9 The *Pennsylvania Packet* is available on microfiche at Stanford University, California.

10 Billy G. Smith and Richard Wojtowicz, *Blacks Who Stole Themselves, Advertisements for Runaways in the Pennsylvania Gazette,* 1728-1790 (Philadelphia: University of Pennsylvania Press, 1989) 136.

11 Ibid.

12 Ibid.

5 A MAN OF COLOUR

1 The settlement that is now the town of Niagara-on-the-Lake will be referred to simply as Niagara, the name the location had for much of its existence. In the local Iroquoian language, the awe-inspiring water falls was named "Onghiara," a word that the French heard as Niagara, and this becme the European name for both the falls and the river. The French built a post on the east side of the mouth of the river called Fort Niagara, a name which was retained when the British captured the fort in 1759. After 1783 and the loss of the east bank of the Niagara River to the United States (although Fort Niagara would be held until 1795), the settlement around Butler's Barracks was known by a number of names. These included Loyal Village, Butlersburg and West Niagara. The village was briefly the capital of the new colony of Upper Canada under the name of Newark. When the capital was shifted to York after 1796, the name of the town was again changed to Niagara. In 1812, Niagara remained as the most important community in the region. The area that would become the city of Niagara Falls was, at that time, fields, farmland and bush. The name was changed to Niagara-on-the-Lake in the early 1900s by the post office in order to avoid confusion between the two locations, when delivering the mail.2. Janet Carnochan, *History of Niagara.* (Toronto: William Briggs, 1914) 7.3.

Nancy Butler and Michael Power, *Slavery and Freedom in Niagara*, (Niagara-on-the-Lake: The Niagara Historical Society, 1993) (Niagara-on-the-Lake: The Niagara Historical Society, 1993) 14.

4 Daniel G. Hill, *The Freedom Seekers*. (Toronto: The Book Society of Canada, 1981) 9; and Robin W. Winks, *The Blacks In Canada*. (Montreal: McGill-Queen's University Press, 1971) 34.

5. Winks, 34.

6. Butler and Power, 12.

7 William Loren Katz, *Breaking the Chains*. (New York: Atheum, 1990) 19.

8 Angela E. M. Files, "Bondage to Freedom–The Black Loyalists of Upper Canada," *The Loyalist Gazette, Fall 1991*. (Toronto: The United Empire Loyalists' Association of Canada, 1991) 36.

9 Katz, 101.

10 Ibid, 103.

11 Ernest Green, "Upper Canada's Black Defenders," *OHS Papers and Records, Vol. XXVII*. (Toronto: Ontario Historical Society, 1931) 365.

12 Files, 37.

13 Butler and Power, 21.

14 Joan Magee, *Loyalist Mosaic: A Multi-ethnic Heritage*. (Toronto & Charlottetown: Dundurn Press, 1984) 90.

15 All mentions of land grants and related information come from the Archives of Ontario's Land Records. Records for the Crown Lands in Ontario have been kept since the 1780s. They are found in the Archives of Ontario under three record series: RG1 C-I - free grants; RG1 C-II - leases and RG1- C-III -sales. The Land Record Index can be searched both by township or by the person's name. Another record series, RG1 C-IV called the Township Papers, is a miscellaneous collection of documents that was brought together as a means to sort and arrange otherwise orphaned records. If a document mentions a specific lot and contains nothing of general interest, it has been defined as a township paper.
The Township Papers are arranged by township, concession and lot. They contain: copies of Orders-in-Council, location certificates and location tickets, assignments, certificates of settlement duties, copies of receipts, some correspondence (mostly inquiries), copies of Surveyor-General's descriptions, and a few patents.
Jackson, John N. and Wilson, Sheila M., St. Catharines, Canada's Canal City, 20.

16 John N. Jackson and Sheila M. Wilson *St. Catharines, Canada's Canal City* (St. Catharines: The St. Catharines Standard Limited, 1992) 20.

17 Written communication from J.K. Joupien of St. Catharines, Sept. 15, 1999.

18 Archives of Ontario, Land Records,

6 PARTNERS IN OBSCURITY

1 Steve Pitt, "To Stand and Fight Together," *Rotunda, Vol. 29, No. 3, Spring 1997*, 11.

2 W.M. Gray, *Soldiers of the King*. (Erin: Boston Mills Press, 1995) 185-186.

3 Ernest Cruikshank, *History of the Campaign upon the Niagara Frontier, Part IV, October to December, 1812*. (Welland: Lundy's Lane Historical Society, 1902-1908) 162.

4 Pitt, p 11; Ernest Green, "Upper Canada's Black Defenders," *OHS Papers and Records, Vol. XXVII* 365f. The Runcheys also provided a captain, Thomas Runchey, for one of the two African "Coloured" companies raised in Niagara for the Rebellion of 1837. He absconded to the United States in the summer of 1838 with his company's payroll.

5 Ernest Cruikshank, *History of the Campaign upon the Niagara Frontier, Part IV,* 162.

6 Pitt, 12.

7 *History of the County of Middlesex.* (–, 1889, reprinted Belleville: Mika Studio 1972) 147. "Simon Grote, of Longwood (colored), did not recollect his age [of enlistment]; thought that his Colonel was Clause. The whole regiment was composed of colored men, and he enlisted at the beginning of the war, and served through it all; was at Lundy's Lane, Queenston, and St. Davids. he got a hundred acres of land from the Government."

8 Janet Carnochan, *History of Niagara,* 171-172.

9 J.G. Currie, "The Battle of Queenston Heights," *Niagara Historical Society No. 4.* (Niagara: Times Book and Job Print, 1917) –? This sparse reference is the only known, published eyewitness narrative of the Coloured Corps in action.

10 Carl Benn, *The Iroquois in the War of 1812.* (Toronto: University of Toronto Press, 1998) 96; Robert Malconson, "Little Gain at Great Cost: A Canadian View of the War of 1812," *Command Magazine, No. 48,* April 1998, 25.

11 Gary E. French, *Men of Colour.* (Stroud: Kaste Books 1978) 61; Green, 368.

12 Malconson, 29.

13 Gray, 259f. There is a famous case of assumed desertion during the Battle of Waterloo in June, 1815. The 7th Netherlands Militia Battalion, part of the Dutch army allied with the British at the battle, showed 201 men missing when roll call was taken after the fight. British historians have interpreted "missing" as "deserted," and based on this, concocted a story of mass desertion by the Dutch at Waterloo. However, "missing" does not necessarily mean "location unknown," but simply means men not present for duty when a roll call was taken. This could be the result of desertion, but also includes men killed on the battlefield and never found, men taken prisoner, or those absent for any number of reasons. In the case of the men of the 7th Militia, their location was known. They were part of a 400-man detachment sent to the rear to guard a massive column of 3,000 French prisoners. When roll call was taken some hours after the battle, they were still on guard duty, and thus "missing" from the total number of men available for combat. See D. Hamilton Williams, *Waterloo New Perspectives.* (New York: John Wiley and Sons, 1994) for more on the sometimes nebulous nature of military number crunching.

14 Ibid, 249f.

15 Ernest Cruikshank, *Documentary History of the Campaign on the Niagara Frontier, 1814.* (Welland: Lundy's Lane Historical Society 1900) 331.

16 Malconson, 29.

17 Ernest Cruikshank, "The Battle of Stoney Creek and Blockade of Fort George, 1813," *Niagara Historical Society No. 3.* (Niagara-on-the-Lake: Niagara Historical Society, 1897/98) 249ff.

18 Green, 369.
19 Gray, 185-186.
20 Cruikshank, *Documentary History of the Campaign on the Niagara Frontier, 1814.* 51.
21 Ernest Cruikshank, *Drummond's Winter Campaign.* (Welland: Lundy's Lane Historical Society, 1990) 6.
22 Gray, 249f.
23 David Flemming, *Fort Mississauga.* (Ottawa: National Historic Parks and Sites Branch, Parks Canada, 1982) 11.
24 Ernest Cruikshank, *Drummond's Winter Campaign,* 6.
25 Ernest Cruikshank, *Documentary History of the Campaign on the Niagara Frontier, 1814,* 28-29.
26 Ibid. 28-29 and 51.
27 *History of the County of Middlesex,* 147.
28 Malconson, 35.

7 HOME ON THE GRAND

1 Janet Carnochan, *History of Niagara,* 27.
2 Jean R. Burnet, with Howard Palmer, *"Coming Canadians" An Introduction to a History of Canada's Peoples.* (Toronto: McLelland and Stewart with the Ministry of Supply and Services, 1988) 18.
3 Largely unknown, this Queen's Bush settlement was the topic of a master's thesis by Linda Brown-Kubisch at the University of Missouri-Columbia. Three articles were published as a result of her research.
   The Black Experience in the Queen's Bush, Ontario History, Volume LXXXVII, Number 2. (Toronto: Ontario Historical Society, 1996). *The Missionaries in the Black Settlement of the Queen's Bush, Wellington County History, Vol. 9.* (Fergus, Wellington County Historical Society, 1996).
   Fugitive Slaves and Free-Americans in Canada West Before 1860, Families, Vol. 35, No. 4. (Toronto: Ontario Genealogical Society, 1996).
4 Oro Township is part of Simcoe County; Artemesia Township is in Grey County.
5 Archives of Ontario, Land Records.
6 Headley Tulloch provides a copy of the petition in *Black Canadians* (Toronto: New Canada Publications, 1975) 98. The original petition is in the National Archives of Canada.
7 Ibid, 98.
8 Mono Township is in Dufferin County.
9 Fergus is located in what was Nichol Township Wellington County. Garrafraxa Township was located immediately east of Nichol.
10 Archives of Ontario, Land Records.
11 National Archives of Canada, RG 8C, Volume 1700, Reel C-4305.
12 Pat Mattaini Mestern, *Fergus: A Scottish Town by Birthright.* (Toronto: Natural Heritage/Natural History Inc., 1995) 38. While working on the Sequicentennial history book on Fergus, *Looking Back, The Story of Fergus Through The Years, 1833-1983,* Pat Mestern was in contact with Mrs. Herbert Corcoran. Mrs. Corcoran, a granddaughter of James Webster, had in her possession family correspondence

which included references to Deaf Moses and his ride with the Webster family in Garafraxa Township. Unfortunately, the whereabouts of the Webster letters is now unknown.

13 Wellington County Museum and Archives, *Dobbin Family History, Volume 3*. Fergus, Ontario.

14 Pat Mestern et al, *Looking Back: The Story of Fergus Through the Years, 1833-1983, Volume 1*. (Fergus: Fergus History Book Committee 1983) 32.

15 Ibid, 51.

16 We have had the opportunity of talking with Howard Sheffield, Yuonne Wilson and Caroline Wilson. Together, they continue to inform the public of Ontario's African legacy through the Sheffield Park Black History and Cultural Museum in Collingwood, Ontario.

17 Archives of Ontario, Land Records.

18 Pat Mestern et al, 55.

8 THE JOURNEY HOME

1 Archives of Ontario, Last will and testament of Richard Pawpine, RG 22-235.

2 Louth Township was directly west of Grantham Township in Lincoln County.

3 Pat Mattaini Mestern, *Fergus: A Scottish Town by Birthright*, 19.

Bibliography

Becker, C., "Kayor and Baol: Senegalese Kingdoms and the Slave Trade in the 18th Century," *Forced Migration,* ed. J.E. Inikori, (ed), Hutchinson University Library for Africa, 1982.

Bell, Herbert C., (Ed.) *History of Northumberland County.* Chicago: Brown, Runk & Co., 1891.

Benn, Carl, *The Iroquois in the War of 1812,* Toronto: University of Toronto Press, 1998.

Burnett, Jean, Butler, Nancy & Power, Michael, *Slavery and Freedom in Niagara,* Niagara-on-the-Lake: The Niagara Historical Society, 1993.

Carnochan, Janet, *History of Niagara.* Toronto: William Briggs, 1914.

Cruikshank, Ernest, *The Battle of Fort George.* Niagara-on-the-Lake: Niagara Historical Society, 1990.

Cruikshank, Ernest, *The Battle of Lundy's Lane.* Welland: Lundy's Lane Historical Society, 1893, reprinted 1984.

Cruikshank, Ernest, "The Battle of Stoney Creek and Blockade of Fort George, 1813," *Niagara Historical Society No. 3.* Niagara-on-the-Lake: Niagara Historical Society, 1897/98.

Cruikshank, Ernest, *Butler's Rangers.* Niagara Falls: Lundy's Lane Historical Society, 1893, reprinted 1988.

Cruikshank, Ernest, *Documentary History of the Campaign on the Niagara Frontier, 1814.* Welland: Lundy's Lane Historical Society, 1900.

Cruikshank, Ernest, *Drummond's Winter Campaign.* Welland: Lundy's Lane Historical Society, 1900.

Cruikshank, Ernest, *History of the Campaign upon the Niagara Frontier, Part II, 1812; Part IV, October - December 1812; and Part VII August - October 1813.* Welland: Lundy's Lane Historical Society, 1902-1908.

Currie, J.G., "The Battle of Queenston Heights," *Niagara Historical Society No. 4.* Niagara: Times Book and Job Print, 1917.

Drew, Benjamin, *The Refugee or the Narratives of Fugitive Slaves in Canada.* Boston: John P. Jewett and Company, Boston, 1856; Toronto: reprinted Coles Publishing Company, 1972.

Files, Angela E.M., "Bondage to Freedom - The Black Loyalists of Upper Canada," *The Loyalist Gazette, Fall 1991.* Toronto: The United Empire Loyalists' Association of Canada, 1991.

Fischer, Joseph R., *A Well Executed Failure.* Columbia: University of South Carolina Press, 1997.

Flemming, David, *Fort Mississauga.* Ottawa: National Historic Parks and Sites Branch, Parks Canada, 1982.

French, Gary E., *Men of Colour.* Stroud: Kaste Books, 1978.

Gomez, Michael A., *Pragmatism in the Age of Jihad, The Precolonial State of Bundu.* Cambridge: Cambridge University Press, 1992.

Grant, Douglas, *The Fortunate Slave.* London: Oxford University Press, 1968.

Gray, W.M., *Soldiers of the King.* Erin: Boston Mills Press, 1995.

Green, Ernest, "Upper Canada's Black Defenders," *OHS Papers and Records, Vol. XXVII.* Toronto: Ontario Historical Society, 1931.

Haight, Canniff, *Country Life in Canada.* Toronto: Hunter, Rose & Co., 1885; Belleville: reprinted Mika Silk Screening Limited, 1971.

Hill, Daniel G., *The Freedom Seekers.* Toronto: The Book Society of Canada, 1981.

––, *History of the County of Middlesex*, 1889; Belleville: reprinted Mika Studio, 1972

Hoyt, Edwin P., *African Slavery.* London and New York: Abelard-Schuman Limited, 1974.

Jackson, John N. and Wilson, Sheila M., *St. Catharines, Canada's Canal City.* St. Catharines: The St. Catharines Standard Limited, 1992.

Jones, Constance, *Africa.* New York: Facts on File, 1993.

Joyner, Charles, *Down by the Riverside.* Urbana and Chicago: University of Illinois Press, 1984.

Katcher, P., *Encyclopedia of British, Provincial and German Army Units 1775-1783.* Harrisburg: Stackpole Books, 1973.

Katz, William Loren, *Breaking the Chains.* New York: Atheneum, 1990.

Malconson, Robert, "Little Gain at Great Cost: A Canadian View of the War of 1812," *Command Magazine, No. 48, April 1998.* San Luis Obispo, 1998.

Martin, E.C., *The British West African Settlements 1750-1821.* London: Longman, Grant and Co., 1927

McManus, Edgar J., *Black Bondage in the North.* Syracuse, Syracuse University Press, 1973.

McManus, Edgar J., *A History of Negro Slavery in New York.* Syracuse: Syracuse University Press, 1966.

Mestern, Pat et al, *Looking Back, The Story of Fergus Through the Years, 1833 - 1983.* Fergus: privately published, 1983.

Mestern, Pat Mattaini, *Fergus: a Scottish Town by Birthright.* Toronto: Natural Heritage/Natural History Inc., 1995.

Minks, Louise, *Traditional Africa*. San Diego, Lucent Books, 1996.

_____, *Molly Brant: Woman of Two Worlds*, State of New York Office of Parks, Recreation and Historic Preservation, (Not dated).

Parnall, Maggie, *Black History in the Niagara Peninsula*. Jordan Station: privately published, 1996.

Pennsylvania Gazette, January 19, 1780 edition.

Pennsylvania Packet and Advertiser, March 13 and 23, 1779 editions.

Piersen, William D., *Black Yankees*. Amherst: The University of Massachusetts Press, 1988.

Pitt, Steve, "To Stand and Fight Together," *Rotunda, Vol. 29, No. 3, Spring 1997*. Toronto: Royal Ontario Museum, 1997.

Reynolds, Edward, *Stand the Storm, A History of the Atlantic Slave Trade*. London: Allison and Busby Limited, 1985.

Riendeau, Roger, *An Enduring Heritage*. Toronto: Dundurn Press, 1984.

Rinaldi, Ann, *Hang a Thousand Trees with Ribbons: The Story of Phillis Wheatley*. Dan Diego/New York/London: Harcourt, Brace & Company, 1996.

Searing, James F., *West African Slavery and Atlantic Commerce: The Senegal River Valley, 1700-1860*. Cambridge: Cambridge University Press, 1993.

Smith, Billy G. and Wojtowicz, Richard, *Blacks Who Stole Themselves, Advertisements for Runaways in the Pennsylvania Gazette, 1728-1790*. Philadelphia: University of Pennsylvania Press, 1989.

Smy, William A., "By Beat of Drum," *The Loyalist Gazette, December 1985*. Toronto: The United Empire Loyalists' Association of Canada, 1985.

Tulloch, Headley, *Black Canadians*. Toronto: New Canada Publications, 1975.

Wallace, Anthony F.C., *The Death and Rebirth of the Seneca*. New York: Alfred A. Knopf, 1969.

Walvin, James, *Black Ivory: A History of British Slavery*. London: HarperCollins, 1992.

Watt, Gavin K., *The Burning of the Valleys: Daring Raids from Canada against the New York Frontier in the Fall of 1780*. Toronto: Dundurn Press, 1997.

Wilson, Sherrill D., *New York City's African Slaveowners*. New York and London: Garland Publishing, Inc., 1994.

Winks, Robin W., *The Blacks in Canada*. Montreal: McGill-Queen's University Press, 1971.

Woolley, Allan, *Butler's Rangers, Crown Forces in America 1775-1783*. http://iaw.on.ca/awoolley/brang/brang.html, 1998.

Wright, Donald, *African Americans in the Colonial Era: From African Origins through the American Revolution*. Arlington Heights: Harlan Davidson, Inc., 1990.

Illustration Credits

1 THE WELLSPRING

Page 18, Originally in *Travels in Western Africa* by Major William Gray and the late Staff Surgeon Douchard, 1825.

Page 21, Originally in *Travels into the Inland Parts of Africa* by Francis Moore, 1738.

Page 24, North Carolina Collection, University of North Carolina Library at Chapel Hill.

Page 25, Iain Fairweather, CDP NETworks.

2 THE TIME OF TERROR

Page 30, Originally in *Broken Shackles* by Glenelg (John Frost), Toronto: William Briggs, 1889.

Page 31, Originally in some memoirs of *The Life of Job* by Thomas Bluett, 1734.

Page 35, Barrington Robinson, after Charles William Peale, 1819.

3 A PIECE OF PROPERTY

Page 38, Originally in *Broken Shackles* by Glenelg (John Frost), Toronto: William Briggs, 1889.

Page 40, Mystic and More Convention and Visitors Bureau.

Page 46, Painting attributed to Sir Edmund Wyly Grier, c.1896. Toronto Reference Library, J. Ross Robertson Collection, T15273.

Page 48, Toronto Reference Library, T31903.

Page 50, Peter Meyler.

4 THE RHYTHM OF WAR

Page 55, Peter Meyler.

Page 59, Peter Meyler.

Page 62, Stanford University.

Page 63, Peter Meyler.

Page 66, Peter Meyler.

Page 67, After Isaac Weld, 1796. Toronto Reference Library, T32170.

5   A MAN OF COLOUR

Page 73, Peter Meyler.
Page 75, St. Catharine's Museum, St. Catharine's Ontario.
Page 76, Attributed to John Wesley Cotton, c.1913. Toronto Reference Library, MTL2686.
Page 77, Toronto Reference Library, T13489.
Page 78, C.W. Jeffries.
Page 79, St. Catharine's Museum.

6   PARTNERS IN OBSCURITY

Page 82, Peter Meyler.
Page 84, Peter Meyler.
Page 89, Attributed to Sir Edmund Wyly Grier, c.1896. Toronto Reference Library, J. Ross Robertson Collection, T15265.
Page 90, Peter Meyler
Page 94, Peter Meyler.
Page 97, Peter Meyler.

7   HOME ON THE GRAND

Page 103, Peter Meyler.
Page 105, Peter Meyler.
Page 107, Archives of Ontario, RG1-100 (94) detail.
Page 109, Peter Meyler.
Page 111, Attributed to Owen Staples c.1913.

8   THE JOURNEY HOME

Page 114–115, Archives of Ontario, RG22-235.
Page 116, Wellington County Museum and Archives.
Page 117, Toronto Reference Library, J. Ross Robertson Collection, T15185.

Page 139, Peter Meyler.

Index

IN MEMORY OF OFFICERS, NON-COM-
MISSIONED OFFICERS AND MEN WHO
WERE KILLED, DIED OF WOUNDS AND DIS-
EASE, IN THE FOLLOWING REGIMENTS
OR COMPANIES OF REGIMENTS ENGAGED
DURING THE WAR OF 1812-1815 UPON THE
WESTERN CANADIAN FRONTIER, WEST OF
KINGSTON.

ROYAL ARTILLERY   ROYAL ENGINEERS
19TH DRAGOONS 41ST REGIMENT 100TH REGIMENT
1ST REGIMENT 49TH „ 103RD „
6TH „ 82ND „ 104TH „
8TH „ 89TH „
ROYAL VETERAN REGT.   SIMCOE MILITIA
„ NEWFOUNDLD „ GLENGARY FENCIBLES „
PROV. DRAGOONS MILITIA YORK RANGERS „
WATTSVILLE REGT. „ 1ST NORFOLK „
CANADIAN FENCIBLES „ COLOURED CORPS & INDIANS

ABOUT THE AUTHORS

Peter Meyler   **David Meyler**

Peter and David Meyler, the sons of Dutch immigrants, were born in the small southwestern Ontario town of Fergus. They spent most of their childhood just outside of town, in West Garafraxa Township. Numerous family trips to historic sites throughout Ontario generated an interest in the history and cultures of the people who settled here.

Peter followed his aptitude for the visual arts by attending Sheridan College in Oakville, Ontario where he earned his diploma in Graphic Design. He now lives in Orangeville, Ontario with his wife Wendy and their daughters Lacadia and Laynna. He operates his own business providing services in graphic design, forms management and writing. Peter has written numerous articles on Ontario's history.

David pursued his interest in history by studying at the University of Toronto. A member of the Dean's list, he received his master's degree in 1982. After working as an editor and writer in the travel industry, David switched careers by earning his Bachelor of Education from the University of Western Ontario. He currently teaches for the Toronto Board of Education. His wife Susan and daughter Emma complete his household in Toronto. His interest in military history has allowed him to be a regular contributor to *Command* magazine.